# TOOTING MOON

### A DUSTY KENT MYSTERY

## By
## Brigid George

Published by Potoroo Press 2020
Albert Park, Victoria, Australia, 3206

Copyright © 2020 by Brigid George

*Tooting Moon* is book #5 in the Dusty Kent Mysteries following *Murder in Murloo*, *A Devious Mind*, *Rippling Red* and *Disguising Demons*.

This is a work of fiction. Apart from historical references, names, characters and incidents are either the product of the author's imagination or are used fictitiously, and any resemblance to actual persons, living or dead, or to actual events is entirely coincidental.

**Please note:** This eBook uses British English spelling. Readers who are used to American English might notice a difference in the spelling of some words. For example: centre (instead of center), colour (instead of color), realise (instead of realize), travelled (instead of traveled).

**Print Edition**

# CHAPTER 1

I WAS ON Sindbad's back ready for my ride. Instead of getting up from his sitting position as he was supposed to, the camel turned his head in my direction and bellowed a snort of protest. Lugubrious brown eyes stared at me from behind great wide nostrils that resembled portals to secret caves. This dromedary didn't like me. What was his problem? A prejudice against Irishmen?

Relaxing my grip on the saddle handles, I turned to tell the tour guide I was getting off. That's when Sindbad rose with sudden and unexpected speed. One minute the camel was on the sand, legs curled under his body. The next minute he'd sprung to full height.

"He's the tallest camel on Cable Beach." This had been the proud declaration of Hugh, a tanned and muscular Australian tour guide in his early thirties, when he introduced me to Sindbad. At the time, having only seen the camel seated, I thought Hugh was exaggerating. He wasn't.

My stomach lurched. I toppled to one side. I think I yelled. Or screamed. Or swore. Probably all three. The next minute I was flat on my back on the sand. All six feet of me spread lengthwise like a misplaced cadaver.

One of the cameleers, a cheerful blue-eyed blonde in her twenties who had earlier introduced herself as Iris, ran over to me. I managed to scramble to my feet before she had a chance to check my pulse.

"Are you all right?" Her tone was serious, her expression concerned, but she couldn't hide the hint of amusement in her eyes.

"Nothing broken." I reassured her as I retrieved my brand new Akubra hat which had become separated from my head during my descent. I brushed the sand from the back of my shorts. Luckily the beach had provided a soft landing.

With the delicacy of a trained handler, Iris coaxed Sindbad into a sitting position again. I ignored the waiting back of the camel and looked up at Dusty, astride a dromedary called Aladdin and looking cool and relaxed in a pair of turquoise cotton shorts and white strappy top. She made no effort to hide her amusement. Even Aladdin appeared to have merriment in his sultry brown eyes.

"I think I'll pass on the camel ride." I tried to sound nonchalant.

Sindbad turned his head in my direction, his mouth wide open. His fat lower lip flopped down to expose square yellow teeth that looked like three inch high tombstones. I recoiled.

"Don't worry," said Dusty. "Camels are herbivores."

I gave her a look which I hoped expressed my scorn for her flippancy. Dusty tossed her head back and laughed.

"Come on, Sean. A sunset camel ride in Broome is an iconic tourist attraction. You don't want to miss out."

It had been almost a year since Dusty Kent and I worked our last case together in Port Douglas. Four years ago, just after I arrived in Australia from Ireland, Dusty took me on as her assistant after learning about my IT qualifications. An investigative journalist, she had already established a reputation for solving the cold case murders she wrote about. In fact, she had solved every case she'd accepted. My role as research assistant had broadened into adviser, listener and friend during our travels to various Australian cities to solve murders. Now we were over two thousand kilometres north of the Western Australian capital of Perth.

I was about to reply that any interest I might have had in this iconic experience had vanished when Sindbad, sounding like a baritone bull with a sore throat, bellowed with the triumph of a conqueror.

That did it! I wasn't going to let a dromedarian Shrek get the better of me. I put my foot in the stirrup and took a firm hold of the saddle handles. Iris was quickly at my side supporting my back with her hand.

"You need to sit down very gently," she urged in a soft voice.

"Then you won't spook the camel."

So it was my fault Sindbad got spiteful? My fault he didn't like the way I sat in the saddle chair? I held on tight to the handles, swung my leg over the camel's back and lowered myself into the saddle.

"Perfect." Iris gave me the thumbs-up.

No reaction from Sindbad. But I didn't trust him. I sensed he would take the first opportunity to assert his dominance.

Hugh appeared on the other side of Sindbad with some last minute instructions for me on how to stay safe during the camel's ascent to full height.

After a glance in my direction to check if I was ready, Iris gave Sindbad the command to rise. I held my breath, leaned back as instructed and gripped the handles. The camel half rose on his front knees, at the same time extending his back legs to full length for support then straightening his front legs to stand on all fours. Smooth. Graceful. Trouble free. I relaxed a little but remained on guard against further tomfoolery from the contemptuous camel.

"Bravo," said Dusty.

We were soon on our way. Cable Beach is a twenty-two kilometre stretch of white sand bounded by sand dunes and ochre red cliffs that runs along the edge of the Indian Ocean. Already on the beach were long caravans of camels with eager riders on their backs. Dusty had booked a private tour so it was just the two of us riding side by side with the handlers leading Aladdin and Sindbad.

"Are you sure camels are herbivores?"

"Yep. It's true." Dusty's response had the earnest ring of sincerity. "On the other hand..." Now she looked at me with an all too familiar mischievous sparkle in her eye. "I read an article the other day about a man in India having his head bitten off by his camel."

"Jaysis!"

"The poor camel had good reason for its behaviour. The owner had left him tied up in the searing heat for hours."

"Right. Sounds like he deserved to lose his head." But who could predict what a camel might deem as 'good reason' to chomp a person's head off? Sindbad managed to take offence simply because I didn't sit on him with the required amount of gentleness. I maintained a watchful eye on the back of Sindbad's head as our camels galumphed along the white sand accompanied by the sound of waves crashing into shore. The camel caravans ahead of us created long shadows on the sand as the sun began to set across the water.

To my amazement, I saw several people strolling along the beach without a stitch of clothing on.

Noticing my reaction, Dusty smiled. "This is the nudist end of Cable Beach."

That some of the naked bodies were not unpleasant to my eye was an agreeable surprise. I apparently slipped into a deep state of concentration. We'd travelled some distance before I heard Dusty cough. She grinned when I turned toward her.

"Do you know how long I've been trying to get your attention?"

"What do you mean?"

My innocent tone caused her to raise her eyebrows.

I attempted to justify my distracted state. "Right. Well, the view…I mean, you're correct. It would have been a shame to miss this iconic experience."

Dusty chuckled. "It's not the only reason I summoned you to Broome."

I didn't know anything about the murder we were to be working on. In her email, Dusty had simply described it as 'an extraordinary case' promising to 'reveal all' when I arrived.

Without waiting for an answer, Dusty continued. "We're here to nail a mongrel who murdered his wife."

Her sharp tone surprised me. Was there something personal about this case? Her profile gave nothing away. The setting sun added a warm glow to her features and deepened the auburn of her frizzy hair which today she wore loose.

"Right. So we know who the murderer is already?"

"Yes, we do." Dusty's lips set in a firm line. "None other than Blake Montgomery."

"Blake Montgomery? The Hollywood actor?"

Sindbad discharged a loud warning snort. My surprise must have caused me to move inappropriately in the saddle. Iris soothed the camel with soft words of reassurance.

"The very one," said Dusty. "The famous Hollywood actor."

The death of Blake Montgomery's wife Tirion Welsh, affectionately known as Tiri, had been big news when it happened. She was the toast of Hollywood and considered one of the most beautiful women in the world. In fact, Blake and Tiri were Hollywood's golden couple, both of them big stars in their own right. Whenever possible, they escaped from the media and the fans on their private yacht. Once a year they sailed to the west coast of Australia to visit Tiri's sister in Broome. On one such visit seventeen years ago Tiri Welsh drowned at sea when she fell overboard. Her death was ruled an accident but Tiri's adoring fans hadn't accepted Montgomery's story that his wife had fallen overboard.

As the camels continued their slow meander along the beach, we admired the spectacular colours created by the warm orange sun lowering itself toward the horizon. Silhouettes of several people standing at the water's edge, fishing rods extended over the water, foreshadowed the advent of nightfall. They all appeared to be wearing at least one piece of clothing. However, the occasional naked body could still be spied on the beach.

We arrived at the finish of the sunset tour without any further shenanigans from Sindbad. He appeared to have accepted me now I had learned how to behave in the saddle.

When the camels came to a halt, Dusty was the first to dismount. Aladdin lowered himself to his front knees, folded his back legs under his body and settled onto his stomach on the sand in what seemed like one smooth movement. Dusty got off his back just as effortlessly, giving the camel a caress before stepping away and looking up at me.

"Finding out what really happened the night Tiri Welsh died could turn out to be a tough case to crack," I said, looking down at her from Sindbad's back.

I knew Dusty's absolute confidence in her ability to solve the cold cases she accepted was legitimised by her one hundred percent success rate. However, the death of Tiri Welsh was pretty much an open and shut case of accidental drowning with no way of proving otherwise.

Instead of replying, Dusty took out her phone and held it up ready to take a photo of me as I alighted from Sindbad. This might not be a picture I would be proud of. When the camel lowered himself to the ground without mishap, I breathed a sigh of relief and dismounted.

Sindbad got up almost immediately, perhaps keen to go home. Grateful to the animal for carrying me safely, I reached out to stroke his neck. Sindbad turned his head toward me and brought his face close to mine. I jumped back. This beast and I might have established friendly relations but I drew the line at kissing! To my surprise, those flappy camel lips bypassed my mouth and went straight to my hat. Before I knew what was happening, Sindbad had gripped the brim of my Akubra in his cenotaphic teeth, whipped it off my head and galloped away.

Iris yelled after him. "Sindbad! Come back!"

The camel paid no heed. Iris gave chase.

"Don't worry. We'll get your hat back." Hugh's apologetic expression was not as solemn as it could have been.

Dusty held her phone up. "I've got it all on film."

"Right. Useful evidence for when I take the camel to court."

As we watched Iris pursuing Sindbad along the beach, Dusty responded to my earlier remark about the cold case.

"It's not Tiri Welsh's death we're here to investigate. Blake Montgomery's second wife was murdered six months ago."

# CHAPTER 2

AFTER RETRIEVING MY hat from an apologetic Iris, Dusty and I had returned to the beach house where we were staying before she was ready to give me further details of our investigation. The split-level house was a short walk from the beach and surrounded by leafy tropical trees. Inside, the house's simplicity was enhanced with an open plan design and floor-to-ceiling glass along the front. Elegant sofas were strategically positioned to take advantage of the panorama outside. Off the spacious modern kitchen was a gleaming bar area.

"You know I can't work on an empty stomach," Dusty said, after we'd both showered and changed. Producing a bottle of gin from a cabinet in the bar, she grinned. "This is what the ocean at Cable Beach reminds me of."

"Gin?"

"The gorgeous colour of the bottle. Look." She held the bottle of gin aloft. I agreed; the blue tint of the bottle did match the turquoise of the ocean. Knowing Dusty had a penchant for that colour, I risked teasing her.

"So that's why you drink gin and tonics. It's the colour of the bottle you're attracted to."

Dusty responded with a look of mock scorn as she sat down at the glass-topped table nearby. "There's tonic and lemons in the fridge, Mr Barman." Long turquoise earrings accentuated her green eyes. Her petite five-foot-two frame was now sheathed in a red sarong patterned with white flowers. She had twisted her unruly hair into a knot on top of her head although several auburn spirals hung loose around her face. A random beam of light underscored the spattering of freckles on the bridge of her nose.

When I first arrived in Australia, I worked for a short time in hospitality. Although Dusty calls me Mr Maze Master because my degree in electronic engineering from Dublin University had resulted in strong IT skills, she sometimes joked she'd offered me the job as her research assistant because of my ability to make a good gin and tonic. I had mixed drinks for her in the seaside village of Murloo, in Byron Bay, in the northern capital of Darwin and most recently in Port Douglas where Dusty had unmasked the cold-hearted killer of a gentle monk. Dusty approached each case with an indomitable belief in her ability to catch the murderer.

The well-stocked bar even had cans of Guinness. Just as I finished mixing our drinks, we heard a knock on the door accompanied by a call of "Knock knock".

I looked up at the double glass doors but the evening vista of trees and beach was uninterrupted. Whoever had knocked had slipped out of sight. Apparently recognising the voice, Dusty's eyes lit up. A smile spread across her face as she answered.

"Who's there?"

"Jack."

"Jack Who?"

"Not Jack Hoo, Jack Aroo!"

I had learned enough about Australian expressions to recognise the play on words. A jackaroo is someone who works on an outback sheep or cattle station. The female equivalent is jillaroo.

Dusty laughed and clapped her hands. "Jack!"

In answer to the summons, a strange apparition appeared in the doorway. At least, what seemed to me to be a strange apparition. On closer inspection I saw it was a woman; a thin woman, roughly fifty years old, dressed in flowing, multicoloured tie-dyed clothes reminiscent of the hippie era. In contrast to the casual freedom of her attire, her hair was short, white, jelled into sharp peaks and encircled with an orange headband.

Dusty leapt from her seat and ran forward, arms outstretched. As they moved in for an embrace, the hippie gestured at her breasts and said, "Don't hold me too tight." She extracted herself from the hug to swivel around, arms flailing like a child unable to contain her excitement.

"So good to see you, Kent." She danced around the room, robes swirling. Her use of Dusty's surname seemed to be a term of endearment.

Dusty laughed and turned to me. "Sean, this is a totally crazy friend of mine called Jack."

Right. So her name really was Jack. Perhaps it had been shortened from Jackie. What was she doing here? Dusty didn't usually mix her social life with business. When she took on a cold case she gave it her full attention and was rarely distracted by anything else.

Jack danced over to where I was standing to shake hands. She looked up, appraising me with blue eyes not unlike that of a Siamese cat.

"Right on time for a drink, Jack," said Dusty.

Jack opted for a cold beer. She watched as I poured beer from a can, nodding with approval as I guided the amber liquid against the side of the glass to ensure a rich collar of foam at the top.

"Righto, Kent. What's this case you want me to help you with?" Help us with the case? Dusty had said nothing about her to me.

"Remember Tiri Welsh?"

Jack nodded. "Murdered by her husband, Blake Montgomery."

"According to the media. But her drowning was ruled a tragic accident."

Jack rolled her eyes and waited for Dusty to continue.

"Blake Montgomery's second wife was murdered here in Broome a few months ago."

"Fair dinkum?" Jack's hand halted on the way to picking up her glass of beer. "I didn't even know he'd married again, but then I don't keep up with celebrity stuff. Unless it's something sensational like murder." Her hand continued its journey and picked up the beer. She took a swig and added, "So now he's knocked off his second wife, has he?"

"Let's not get ahead of ourselves, Jack. Besides, I haven't even had a chance to tell Sean about you yet." Dusty must have read the confusion on my face as I struggled to work out where Dusty's 'totally crazy' friend fitted in. "I asked Jack to come and use her special skill to help us on this case."

At that moment, Jack's left breast moved.

I blinked and averted my gaze. "Right. Um. Special skill?" Did I really see what I thought I saw? I wasn't about to look at Jack's chest again to find out. Neither of the women seemed to notice my bewilderment.

"Jack has the ability to become invisible." I was pretty sure Dusty didn't mean that literally. I waited for her to explain. Jack got in first.

"I'm a tracker."

"Not like an Aboriginal tracker who can navigate the bush and find people or animals by reading the signs they leave behind," said Dusty. "Jack tracks the behaviour and movements of people in the urban environment. She works freelance for private detectives."

"And sometimes the police." Jack's tone suggested being asked to assist the police was something she considered validation of her abilities.

"Because of her trick of making herself invisible, Jack's one of the best there is at tailing people. Her targets never spot her."

Jack giggled. "Not even when I'm right in front of them sometimes."

"I'm hoping Jack can use her skill to get something on Blake Montgomery. Has he got a new lady friend? Is he violent or controlling? You know the sort of thing."

"If there's anything to be got, I'll get it. No wucking furries!" It took me a few minutes to realise Jack hadn't said what I thought she'd said. My startled reaction caused her to break out in a peal of laughter.

"A good Aussie expression." She winked and took another swig of beer. "Haven't you heard it before?"

Dusty chuckled. "That's another task you can help me with, Jack. I've pledged to Aussify this Irishman." They clinked glasses to seal the deal. "It shouldn't be too difficult. Sean actually has a few Aussie genes."

In answer to Jack's raised eyebrows, I explained. "Recently I found out my mother's great grandmother was Australian." I was in contact with several distant cousins via social media although I had not met any of them in person.

Jack raised her hand to give me an enthusiastic high five. Keeping my eyes from straying to Jack's chest area proved difficult. I couldn't help noticing her left breast seemed fuller than her right one. Maybe she was the unfortunate victim of breast cancer and had had surgery. But that wouldn't explain the movement I saw.

"As a matter of fact," said Dusty, "Sean's a tracker too. Only he's a cyber tracker."

Jack reached over to give me another high-five. "With two trackers on the job we'll crack this case in no time." Her expression became serious. "If there's one thing I can't stand, it's gutless skunks who use physical violence on women." The lightness had gone from her voice. She stared at the opposite wall. When she came out of her reverie, Jack exchanged a meaningful glance with Dusty.

"I agree." Dusty looked across at me, disgust etched in her expression. "Men like that are the lowest of the low."

"Why are you looking at me?" I felt as though I was being accused.

Dusty leaned across to lightly pat the back of my hand by way of reassurance. "Sorry, Sean. I wasn't pointing the finger at you. Not for one second." She turned to Jack. "Sean's one of the good guys."

Jack raised her glass and tilted it in my direction.

"Luckily," continued Dusty, "good guys outnumber the skunks."

"Thank jolly goodness." Jack licked the beer froth from her upper lip.

"By the way, you're a day early. Why didn't you wait for me to send you a plane ticket?"

"Had an offer I couldn't refuse." Jack grinned at us. "This guy I know in Perth lent me a beetle." For a split second I thought she might have taken something that caused her to hallucinate about flying on the back of a beetle, but I quickly realised what she meant.

"A Volkswagen Beetle?"

"Right on, Seamus."

"Sean." Dusty corrected her.

Jack grinned. "Just teasing. What's in a name, eh?"

Dusty put her hand over Jack's in a comforting gesture which piqued my interest. I guessed this was linked to the sombre moment they'd shared a few minutes earlier. Something to do with Jack's name? Or something to do with what I'd occasionally heard Dusty refer to as 'secret women's business'?

# CHAPTER 3

"OKAY, TEAM. LET'S look at our case." Dusty pulled her tablet towards her and swiped it to raise the documents she wanted. I resigned myself to a late dinner, opened a large packet of potato chips and topped up our drinks.

"We're here to investigate the death of Fern Parkes, Blake Montgomery's second wife," continued Dusty. "Fern was forty-one years old. Born in Carolina, USA. Divorced her first husband in 2000. Married Montgomery in 2002. Gave birth to their first child the same year. Fern's acting career had started to take off but after her marriage she gave up acting."

"His idea, I betcha." Jack screwed up her face in contempt. "Didn't want his wife getting too much attention."

"Possible. He might have been feeling insecure. His career was floundering after taking a nosedive when Tiri died."

The police might have exonerated Blake Montgomery but public opinion had labelled him a murderer. After rumours surfaced of a dark side to the golden couple's relationship, suspicion circled Tiri's husband like vultures above a dying cowboy in the desert. Eventually, just like the cowboy, Montgomery died. As an actor, that is. Hollywood's most sought after leading man was reduced to accepting bit parts.

"After she gave up acting," Dusty glanced down at the case file, "Fern started a wellness centre in Los Angeles and later opened one here in Broome."

"Why here, eh? I mean, why'd they leave the glamour and glitz of Hollywood to live in Broome?" Jack's question echoed my own thoughts.

"Exactly." Dusty gave Jack a knowing look. "Why did Blake and Fern come to Broome to live? It should have been the last place where Blake would want to settle. A coastal town in Western Australia with a population of less than fifteen thousand is a long way from the life he's used to. More importantly, it's the place where his first wife died."

"Now it's also the site of his second wife's death," said Jack.

"Yep. And he's still here. It's a bit odd. I mean, he lives on his luxury yacht so it's easy enough for him to go elsewhere. Yet he chooses to stay."

I was beginning to think there was something weird about Blake Montgomery.

"We might be onto something." Dusty's eyes gleamed. "Is there another reason he and Fern came to Broome? Is there something else going on here?"

Jack put her hand up. "Drugs?"

"That's what the police suspected back in 2000 when Tiri drowned," said Dusty. "Blake might still be involved in the drug trade. After all, he seems to have plenty of money even though his career has slumped. Rowley Shoals – where he was the night Tiri died – is a perfect drop off point for drugs because of its remoteness. It's a group of coral atolls about a hundred and sixty nautical miles west of Broome. Maybe his contacts drop off the drugs there in some pre-arranged place. Blake goes and picks them up and brings them into Broome then they're taken by road to Perth. He might even transport them on the yacht further down the coast to Port Hedland or Geraldton to be taken to Perth from there. Does that sound too far-fetched?"

"Sounds reasonable," I said.

Western Australia's 20 000 kilometres of almost empty coastline was a soft target for drug smugglers who used boats and ships from various countries to bring the contraband ashore. I had come to know something about Western Australia after travelling along the west coast on my Thunderbird motorbike a few years previously.

Dusty continued. "Maybe drug dealing is behind the deaths of Tiri and Fern. What if Tiri found out about Blake's involvement in drugs and he had to keep her quiet? The same thing might have happened with Fern." Dusty inclined her head toward me. "Mr Maze Master, see what you can dig up on Blake Montgomery. Look for anything that might link him to drugs, people he associates with, where he's travelled in his yacht, that sort of thing." She swiped her tablet screen to bring up another document. "And Jack, you'll need to know the name of his boat if you're going to keep a spying eye on him. He got rid of the yacht he and Tiri sailed in and bought a new one. Ah, here it is. His yacht is called *Doris*." She glanced up at us with raised eyebrows. "You'd think if he was going to name it after a woman, he'd call it *Fern*."

"I'm surprised he didn't call it the *Blake Montgomery*." Jack's lip curled in contempt. She seemed to have already made up her mind about Montgomery's guilt. Was that because she believed he'd murdered his first wife? Or was there something more personal tainting her perception?

Memories of the old Doris Day movies I used to watch with my mother prompted me to make a suggestion. "He might have named the yacht after Doris Day like."

Dusty looked at me and grinned. The grin broadened until she burst into laughter.

"That wasn't meant to be funny." I was miffed.

Dusty's laughter subsided. "I'm sorry. I wasn't laughing at you, Sean. It's just that I like it when you talk Irish to me."

"Irish?" I had no idea what she meant.

"You did sound quite Irish like." Dusty grinned and added. "More than usual. Anyway, regardless of who he named his yacht after, he's your first target, Jack; the skipper of the *Doris*." Dusty gave her the details of where the yacht was berthed at Queen City Marina.

I'd been careful to keep my eyes averted from Jack's upper body but I couldn't help noticing, in my peripheral vision, a slight wriggling in her left breast similar to what I'd seen earlier. As far as I could tell, her right breast hadn't moved. Surely it's a bit odd to have one wriggling breast?

"Did Fern disappear over the side of Blake's yacht the same way

Tiri did?" I asked the question partly to distract myself from what was happening in Jack's bra.

"No," said Dusty. "But she died on the Marina not far from where his yacht is moored."

Jack's eyes widened. "Fair dinkum? Did she drown?"

"Nope. Strangled. Fern was ambushed and killed one night when she was walking from the Queen City Marina to the car park. She wasn't actually heading to the parking area. She was going to another yacht at the other end of the Marina." Dusty paused for dramatic effect. "Fern was on her way to meet her lover."

"Aha!" Jack's eyes narrowed into angry slits. "For a certain type of man, that's motive for murder."

"I'm glad you're helping us with this one, Jack. If Blake Montgomery did murder Fern, he's not going to get away with it."

Jack straightened her body and raised her beer. "Too damn right he's not!" Dusty brought her glass up to touch Jack's with a light clink.

"Anyway, we'd better organise some food before I go over the details of the case." Dusty drained the last of her gin and tonic. "You wouldn't think it to look at his lean frame but my blue-eyed Irish assistant needs a lot of fuel. He's been a bit distracted. I reckon hunger is the cause."

Jack giggled. "Hunger isn't the only thing distracting him." She put a hand up to her left breast. Mortification that my efforts to be discreet had been unsuccessful sent a hot blush along my neck. This increased Jack's mirth.

Dusty admonished her. "Jack! Stop teasing Sean."

Jack grinned. "Yeah, I should've put him out of his misery sooner. Sorry, Seamus. I couldn't resist. You'll get used to me."

I wasn't sure I wanted to get used to her or her habit of calling me by the wrong name.

Jack patted her left breast. "I haven't got a wriggly boob. It's Spratt. He sometimes sleeps in my bra during the day. He rarely moves. Then again I'm so used to him, I don't usually notice when he does."

Without a hint of embarrassment, Jack reached into her bra cup and gently withdrew a tiny bundle of grey fur. Hugging it to her body, she caressed it like a mother fondling a newborn.

"This is Spratt. Isn't he the cutest, cutest little creature ever?"

As if in answer to the introduction, the bundle of fur uncurled itself to reveal a pink nose and pointy ears. Dark stripes in its fur ran back from its forehead. Both eyelids opened slowly until protruding round eyes, dark brown in colour, shone through the fur. The tiny animal released a series of short angry bleats, similar to that generated when squeezing a soft toy. Having expressed his displeasure at being removed from his warm nest, he closed his eyes and curled up again.

"Oooh. He's grumpy cos we woke him up." Jack bestowed an indulgent smile on the 'cutest, cutest little creature ever'.

"What is it? Looks like a tiny squirrel."

Jack scoffed at my suggestion. "Squirrel? Get outa here. Spratt's an Australian marsupial. Mind you, he can glide through the air like a flying squirrel. But he's not a member of the squirrel family. Spratt's a sugar glider. He belongs to the possum family. Don't you, little cutie?" She puckered her lips at the miniature marsupial. "He doesn't usually wake up until around ten in the evening. Then he's awake all night cos sugar gliders are nocturnal."

When Dusty and I had been in Byron Bay, I'd heard about Drop Bears plummeting out of trees to ambush people so to meet a possum that flies through the air is par for the course when it comes to Australian marsupials.

"I've kept the back room for you, Jack," said Dusty. "There's a tree right outside for Spratt."

Dusty's room was on the upper level overlooking the pool on one side and the ocean on the other. Mine was downstairs toward the front of the house with, like all the bedrooms, an impeccably designed en suite and a magnificent view. The rear room assigned for Jack opened onto a small verandah shaded by a tree canopy.

Jack thanked Dusty with a nod and carefully placed her pet back into her bra. With Spratt safely tucked up in his day bed, we settled down to the serious business of ordering pizza.

# CHAPTER 4

AFTER AN EARLY breakfast the next morning Dusty and I were on our way to a women's drop-in centre to see Tiri Welsh's sister.

The evening before, we had sat at a table in the outdoor bamboo garden enjoying the balmy tropical breeze. The three of us had consumed two large pizzas and a bottle of wine while Dusty explained how she came to be working on the cold case murder of Fern Parkes.

"After Fern was killed, Tiri Welsh's sister Rhona contacted me again," she had said, leaning back in her chair rubbing her stomach with satisfaction. The smell of baked dough, melted cheese and oregano still lingered in the air.

"Again?" I closed the lids of the cardboard pizza boxes and slid them to the other end of the table.

"Yep. She'd asked me in the past to investigate Tiri's murder but you know how long my waiting list is." Dusty was much sought after by families wanting her to hunt down murderers of loved ones after police investigators had been unable to do so. "Besides, if Tiri's death was murder, the only person who could have done it was the husband. What Rhona wanted was some way to prove it. Considering the circumstances, I felt the police were better placed to do that."

Jack opened her eyes wide in mock surprise. "Not like you to be so modest, Kent."

Dusty laughed and turned to me. "Jack knows me too well. We've been mates for years. I was at the Police Training Academy when we met."

"I was on a short visit to Melbourne at the time," said Jack.

The two women exchanged warm smiles as Dusty continued.

"What I mean is, forensic science was needed to really nail Blake

Montgomery for the murder of his first wife. Unfortunately, the police haven't found any evidence to confirm his guilt. Nevertheless, Rhona has never given up the fight to make him accountable. When his second wife was murdered in January this year she was sure Blake Montgomery had done it. Once again the police were unable to find any evidence to support her belief. But Rhona was determined not to let this chance slip away. She hopes a conviction for his second wife's murder will convince the police to re-examine Tiri's case. So she contacted me again and asked me to investigate Fern's murder."

"You know what?" Jack held up her right index finger and rocked it back and forth to underscore the point she was about to make. "Even though I can't be bothered with celebrity gossip, I did read a lot about the Tiri Welsh murder at the time. One little thing has always stuck in my memory. According to an article I read, Tiri Welsh's sister had it in for Blake Montgomery even before the murder."

"Serious?" Dusty lifted her eyebrows in surprise. "I don't remember reading that."

"It wasn't widely reported. I only saw it once. It stayed with me because I remember being angry that the article was trying to discredit the poor woman who was grieving for her sister by digging up some past animosity between her and her brother-in-law."

"What sort of animosity?"

Jack shrugged. "They hinted Rhona had a personal reason other than love for her sister for trying so hard to get Blake Montgomery put behind bars. It might have been mischief on the part of one particular reporter."

"Every little bit of information could be useful, Jack. It wasn't only Rhona who contacted me. Fern's friend Shama Vellu also sent me an email expressing concerns about Blake possibly being responsible for Fern's death."

"Is Montgomery the only suspect?"

"As far as Rhona is concerned, yes. But you're right, Sean. We need to consider who else might have had a motive for murdering Fern."

"An ex-lover?" suggested Jack.

Dusty nodded. "Or her current lover. They might have had a falling out which escalated into a violent altercation."

"Wouldn't be the first time that's happened." Jack's eyes narrowed.

"Could be a jealous wife. Fern's lover might be married." I knew Dusty was right to focus on men close to Fern. According to statistics the majority of murdered women had been killed by a male. However, I also knew Dusty needed to avoid being too narrow in her focus.

She thrust an approving finger in my direction. "Good point. The killer could be a woman." A thoughtful expression crossed her face. "Maybe a jealous wife or a woman driven by a different kind of jealousy. As a glamorous Hollywood identity in a small town like Broome, Fern could have been a target for a deranged stalker jealous of her apparently perfect life."

Jack shook her head. "A male stalker is a more likely possibility, Kent. And while we're on the subject of possibilities, we shouldn't forget about the drug theory. If Montgomery has been involved in drugs, he might have pissed someone off. Fern's murder could have been retribution. It's the sort of thing drug dealers do. Harm someone you love and threaten to do the same to you. That's how they keep people in line, isn't it?"

"See what you can find out on the street. Sean and I will visit Rhona tomorrow."

# CHAPTER 5

Jack had not joined us this morning. The fewer people in Broome who knew who she was and who she was working with, the better she would be able to remain 'invisible' when necessary. We had parked Dusty's retro Holden FJ and walked along Carnarvon Street. Even though it was not yet eight o'clock, the day's sultry beginning heralded another hot and humid day. Australia's southern states were in the grip of winter at this time of year. In Broome, it was the dry season with temperatures often in the 30s.

Dusty, who didn't seem to feel the heat, strode along checking the numbers on the houses as we passed. As some of them weren't numbered, we kept losing track of where we were. A ladder propped up against the wall of one property gave me an opportunity to tease Dusty. I walked straight underneath it as though I didn't know it was there.

"Sean!"

I pretended I hadn't heard her.

She cried out again. "Sean!"

By this time I was on the other side of the ladder.

"Something wrong?" I kept my expression dead pan.

Realising I had been poking fun at her superstitious nature, she glared at me and walked around the ladder.

"I'm a hero." I grinned at her. "I walked under a ladder and lived to tell the tale."

She threw a rebuke over her shoulder at me as she marched away. "You'll be laughing on the other side of your face when the bad luck starts happening."

Eventually, Dusty stopped outside a long weatherboard building with a verandah all the way along the front. "Here it is!"

The length of the building had probably been achieved by joining two old houses together.

"Look!" Dusty pointed to the verandah roof. It had been designed to look like shells, or several folds of one shell with a gleaming white underside.

"That's massive!"

"Awesome," agreed Dusty. "It's like a bullnose verandah, only in the shape of oyster shells."

Trees marked the start and finish of the verandah and no doubt helped to keep the premises cool. A discreet sign above the front door read: *Pearl's Shell: Daytime Drop-in for Women.*

We stepped inside to a large open space with a cafe on the left and a colourful play area on the right where mothers sat on the sidelines watching their children. A baby crawled on a mat, a couple of toddlers sat nearby stacking plastic blocks while another two played a clumsy tug of war with a long fabric caterpillar.

"Good morning!"

The woman advancing toward us from the kitchen servery area was in her late forties, attractively buxom. She was white from head to toe; starting with the thick blonde hair falling to just below her shoulders to the teardrop-shaped pearl earrings, to the flowing cotton top over loose white pants.

"Dusty Kent, I presume?" She smiled and held out both hands to Dusty. "I'm glad to finally meet you in person and so very grateful to you for coming."

Her accent suggested she wasn't a native Australian. Her mellifluous tones enhanced the warmth of her personality. It took me a few seconds to place the sing-song lilt. Welsh! An appealing blend of Welsh and Australian to be precise. I recalled from media articles that Tiri and her sister had been born in Wales. Tiri had chosen her stage name of Welsh to honour her home country.

"I'm Rhona. Rhona Hutchinson."

She scooped one hand around me in a sort of half embrace. "You must be Sean. Dusty has told me how much she relies on your brilliant skills."

I'd expected the face of Tiri's sister to reflect bitterness or entrenched grief. Rhona Hutchinson's glowing face reflected optimism and vivacity. Like her sister, she was a beauty, although she didn't resemble Tiri in her features.

Rhona gestured at the laughing children. "I love seeing these children so happy, especially knowing how different their situation could be without services like Pearl's Shell to support their mothers."

Dusty's face clouded. "You mean the kids could end up being taken out of their homes by social services?"

"I'm afraid so. It does happen."

"It shouldn't happen." The vehemence in Dusty's voice startled me. Rhona's glance of surprise suggested she had noticed it too.

Dusty quickly recovered herself. "Sorry. I know that's usually a last resort when there's no other choice."

Rhona, sensing the subject had touched a nerve in Dusty, refrained from saying anything further. She took Dusty's arm and led her gently toward the stairs. Dusty was quick to change the subject.

"Your pearls are lovely." She gestured at Rhona's earrings. "I assume the history of pearling in Broome inspired the name Pearl's Shell?"

"Very much so," said Rhona. "Pearling is an integral part of Broome. That's one reason for using pearl in the name but there's a more important reason. It relates to a dark side of pearling; the abuse of women. In the early days, Aboriginal women were exploited through the practice of blackbirding."

"Blackbirding?"

"Ugly word, isn't it? It means kidnapping and selling Aboriginal people to work in the pearl industry."

"Serious? That would have been back when Australia was still part of the British Empire. Are we talking about rich Englishmen?"

"The pearling industry in the 1800s was described as a system of slavery carried out under the protection of the British flag and many of the pearling masters were British Imperialists. But pearling masters came from diverse backgrounds. They all wanted to get the best pearls from the sea no matter what."

"Including taking advantage of vulnerable women."

"I'm afraid so. Hence our use of *Pearl* in the name. It symbolises those women as well as the industry they worked in. The word *shell* implies protection. A shell is a protective outer layer. That's what we try to do here at Pearl's Shell; give women at risk a protective layer by making sure their basic needs are taken care of." Rhona gestured at the stairs. "Please, allow me to show you around."

Upstairs, Rhona escorted us through a lounge area and a 'quiet room' with yoga mats, and indicated two bathrooms and three concave shower enclosures. Her enthusiasm for Pearl's Shell was evident in almost every word she uttered.

Despite her vivacity, at one point Rhona's expression dimmed. She had glimpsed something or someone outside that apparently disturbed her. It was only a flicker in her eyes. I wouldn't have noticed had I not been studying her face at the time. Following her line of sight, I saw the disappearing back of a woman wearing a mustard-coloured top. Was there something about this woman that bothered Rhona?

A man wearing a baseball cap and reflector sunglasses leaned against a tree on the other side of the street, diagonally opposite the drop-in centre. A grey T-shirt fell to just below his waist while black shorts exposed heavily tattooed calves. The man appeared to be looking toward Pearl's Shell. Was he connected to one of the women who came to the centre? A violent partner? An ex-husband who couldn't let go? Before I had time to ponder these questions, Rhona led us downstairs. We followed her out to the back courtyard where ancient trees gave ample shade to the seating area. From one of the trees came a sharp series of tweets. I looked up but the bird responsible was practising its innate art of camouflage.

Rhona smiled. "That's our resident flycatcher; a pretty little bird." As she turned toward the door she paused and took Dusty's arm. "I'm so grateful you agreed to look into Fern's murder."

Dusty's eyes met Rhona's. "If Blake Montgomery murdered his wife, I'll make sure he doesn't get away with it."

"Oh, he murdered Fern all right. Just like he murdered my sister."

# CHAPTER 6

"TELL ME ABOUT Tiri," said Dusty.

Tenderness softened Rhona's face. "Tiri and I didn't have any other siblings. You can imagine how close we were."

"She was your big sister?"

"And my fierce protector." Rhona smiled, a nostalgic glaze in her eyes. "Tiri was like a natural pearl, a wild sea pearl, with the same sort of incandescent lustre and flawless complexion. A Sanskrit scholar once told me people in ancient India believed a pearl was made of dewdrops from heaven, fertilized by a flash of lightning to become the daughter of the moon. Like the moon, pearls are feminine and mysterious elements of the universe. Tiri had the same feminine mystique." Rhona beamed with pride.

"That's why you wear pearls; to honour your sister?" Dusty glanced down at her turquoise sandals. She always wore something turquoise in memory of her mother who loved the colour.

"Yes." Rhona caressed her earrings. "Her beauty was unique. He had no right to take that away."

"I know this must be difficult for you to talk about, but it would help me to have some insight into your sister's marriage." Rhona nodded her understanding. Dusty continued. "After Tiri died, rumours circulated that Blake had been physically violent toward her during their marriage. You spoke out about it in a couple of interviews."

"I certainly did!"

"As I understand it, you didn't actually witness Blake being abusive."

"He's too wily to do it in front of witnesses. On one occasion when they were visiting Broome, Tiri rushed over to my place in a state of terror. She was so scared of Blake she insisted on staying the night."

"Tiri didn't tell you he'd been physically abusive toward her on a regular basis?"

"She told me he'd often erupt into violent rages. When I asked her about physical abuse she always denied it. That doesn't mean anything. Abused women often won't admit to being beaten. I should have questioned her more instead of respecting her privacy." Rhona sighed. "I accept it's virtually impossible to prove Blake Montgomery murdered my sister. If he's convicted of Fern's murder, that will be some sort of justice."

The distinctive smell of coffee drifted through the open doorway from the cafe.

Rhona ushered us inside. "Let's finish our tour. We can talk further over a cappuccino."

Facilities downstairs included a laundry, an art and craft room and a well-equipped kitchen. I smelt recently cooked toast and fried bacon. A plump woman with limp blonde hair going dark at the roots stirred the contents of a large pot with a wooden spoon. Steam rose from several other saucepans on the stove top. The woman greeted us with a wave of the spoon when Rhona introduced her as 'Tavish, our chef'.

"Don't ask me how I got my name," growled the chef. "I'm over it!"

Rhona laughed. "Tavish is sick of people asking her how she came by her unusual name, partly because she doesn't know herself." Tavish affected an exasperated expression and put her free hand up to indicate she didn't want to enter into the discussion. "So when people ask me how she got her name," continued Rhona, "I tell them she's a descendant of a great Scottish warlord of the MacTavish clan and was named after him."

Tavish scowled. "Don't ask me to cook haggis."

Rhona smiled. "There's no haggis but we provide breakfast and lunch for the women. Good healthy food is so important."

"My Nan used to say the world always seems brighter on a full stomach," said Dusty.

"So true." Rhona agreed. "Imagine what a difference nutritious meals make to women who are living on the street or going through a difficult time in the home."

"Difficult time!" Tavish snorted and chopped a carrot into pieces with vicious thrusts of the knife. "Hell, more like!"

"Tavish knows what the women go through; they often tell her their stories."

The cook looked up and glared at me, chopping knife raised. "And if any so-called man treated me like that he'd know about it!" She brought the knife down, halving the last carrot with a sharp split along its length. I winced. Tavish knew how to get a message across.

Rhona ushered us to a window table in the cafe area and went over to the espresso machine to make our coffees.

As we sat down, I noticed the tattooed man was still across the street, still leaning against the same tree, arms folded. I wondered whether he might be Tavish's husband but dismissed the thought as soon as it arrived. Any man married to Tavish wouldn't dare to exhibit the arrogance this individual seemed to possess. There was something intimidating about the way he stood. Dusty apparently hadn't noticed him.

The front door opened to admit an attractive dark-skinned woman. Her curvaceous body moved with graceful fluidity as she made her way across to a locker cabinet at the back of the room, waving to the children in the play area as she passed. She placed her handbag in one of the lockers, stowing the key in the top pocket of her red shirt. After the two women exchanged greetings at the coffee machine, Rhona returned to our table, carrying a tray with three steaming mugs.

Dusty accepted one of the mugs of coffee. "Are you the manager of Pearl's Shell?"

Rhona shook her head, causing her earrings to catch the light momentarily. "I'm a gemologist, specialising in pearls, or gems of the moon as I like to think of them. That's how I ended up in Broome. My husband is Australian, a pearler here. When we met in the UK he told me Broome was the perfect place for a pearl specialist." She placed a mug of coffee n front of me. "It was a persuasive argument to convince me to move here. But I'm not sorry to be living in this beautiful place. Who would be? I work with one of the large pearl businesses – taking wealthy clients on private pearl farming tours. When I'm not required at the farm, I'm normally here. I'm a committee member as well as one of the many volunteers."

Rhona deposited the last coffee on the table and stowed the empty tray on one of the vacant chairs. When she sat down, she retrieved a large envelope from her handbag. "I want to show you something." She removed a photograph from the envelope and deposited it on the table.

"Tiri and Blake on their wedding day."

Holding her bouquet in one hand, Tiri looked incandescent, to use Rhona's word, in white with a lace mantilla and long white gloves. Her wavy black hair gleamed. Her dark eyes were fixed lovingly on her new husband. Blake, immaculately dressed in a suit and tie, white shirt and folded white handkerchief in his top pocket, clasped his bride's free hand.

"She looks so happy there, doesn't she?"

Dusty nodded. "It's a cliché, but she's glowing with happiness."

"They make a stunning couple," I said.

"Blake was handsome," added Dusty. "Stand out handsome."

Rhona left the photo face up on the table and arranged another one next to it. She sat back with a knowing look on her face, waiting for us to grasp the significance of the two photos.

# CHAPTER 7

Dusty studied the images. "Is that Fern? Fern and Blake on their wedding day? It's almost the same photo as Tiri and Blake."

Rhona agreed. "Uncanny isn't it, how like Tiri she is?"

"Striking resemblance. Fern could almost pass for her twin." Dusty glanced at Rhona. "Sorry. I didn't mean any disrespect."

Rhona waved aside her apology. "It's true. Fern looked more like Tiri's sister than I do. Tiri took after our dad. I look more like Mum."

Dusty pointed to the second photo. "Fern's obviously quite a bit younger than Blake."

"That's what makes it so spooky. When they got married, Fern was almost the same age as Tiri was when she died. It's like he's trying to prove to himself Tiri is still alive, to convince himself he didn't murder her."

It occurred to me Rhona might be allowing her hatred of Blake to prejudice her thinking. Marrying someone so like his first wife might simply indicate how much Blake missed Tiri. Of course, that didn't exclude him as her killer. I had worked with Dusty long enough to know it was possible for a murderer to genuinely grieve for their dead victim.

"Do you know if a similar pattern of violent rages occurred in his second marriage?"

Rhona rolled her eyes. "A leopard doesn't change his spots."

She inclined her head toward the window as she gathered up the photos. "There's one of our volunteers across the street."

A woman in her early thirties stood outside the General Store dressed in a loose black top and mid-calf leggings that suited her athletic build.

"Her name's Noelene Hyett. She's probably on her way over here."

"Who's that with her?" I asked. A woman in a mustard-coloured top had joined Noelene.

Rhona lowered her voice despite no-one being within earshot. "Muriel Brown. She and Noelene spend a lot of time together." Her brows furrowed. "I think Noelene feels sorry for Muriel."

"How so?"

"Muriel is...well, she's different. She doesn't have many friends. To tell you the truth, I find Muriel a bit...a bit unsettling." Rhona laughed self consciously. "I'm not being very charitable, I know."

"Does she use the services here?" Something about the way Muriel Brown was dressed made me think she might be a woman in need.

"Not anymore. She came here for several months during her marriage break up a few years ago. These days she comes to help out a little bit sometimes. It's kind of her and she seems to genuinely care about supporting other women. Naturally, I make her feel welcome."

The door swung open at that moment. A dynamic energy penetrated the room as Noelene Hyett entered, a draught lifting strands of her straight dark hair from her shoulders. When she saw Rhona, her cheeks dimpled in a smile which softened her stern look. Watching Noelene striding towards us, I imagined her loping along the beach for early morning runs or scaling the rocks at the southern end of Cable Beach.

"Day off today, Noelene?" said Rhona, after she had made the introductions.

"Half day. Thought I'd pop in and help with the kids before I head off to the gym. Brownie has to get the vet out to Benji this morning. Otherwise she'd have come too."

"Brownie is Muriel Brown, Noelene's friend." Rhona's expression revealed no hint of her apprehension about Muriel.

"And Benji?" queried Dusty. "Her dog?"

Noelene smiled. "Brownie's pet camel."

Dusty looked at me, mischief in her eyes. Thankfully she refrained from mentioning my adventure with Sindbad. Noelene declined Rhona's offer of coffee.

"I might have one later – after I've earned it."

She lingered for a moment at our table. I had the impression she wanted to say something to Dusty but after a quick glance at Rhona she decided against it. Instead, she lifted her hand in farewell and made her way to the lockers. More toddlers had now gathered in the play area. Some of the children called out to Noelene.

"Noelene's a Team Leader at Forrest Road Early Learning Centre," explained Rhona. "She often pops in here on her half days to give the mothers a break."

Noelene responded to the children's greetings with a cheery wave. When she sat down on a large red mat and picked up a picture book, the toddlers clamoured around her. She calmed them with an expert touch. They were soon sitting quietly in front of her, faces raised in anticipation.

Dusty turned her attention back to the case. "How well did you know Fern, Rhona?

"Not well at all. I met her once or twice at various functions but we weren't friends or anything."

"You don't socialise with your ex brother-in-law?"

Rhona grimaced. "I despise that man with every fibre of my being."

The intensity of her feelings showed on her face. Dusty leaned toward Rhona, eyes gleaming with catlike interest.

"Did you know Blake before Tiri met him?"

"I did not. I wish my sister had never met him." Rhona blinked away the moisture in her eyes and fell silent. I guessed she was reflecting on what might have been had her sister not fallen in love with Blake. Did she feel regret because she'd been unable to protect her sister? If so, it would explain why her hatred of Blake was so strong. Dusty had not given up on that point.

"What was your relationship with Blake like when he and Tiri first got together?"

Rhona turned her mug back and forth, eyes lowered. Dusty waited. Eventually, Rhona looked up.

"Like everyone else, I thought they were the perfect couple."

Dusty wasn't going to settle for an evasive answer. "Did you like Blake back then?"

A slight pink tinge rushed to Rhona's cheeks. "I had no reason not to. He was charming and seemed to really care about Tiri."

Dusty lowered her voice. "Something happened to change the way you felt about him, didn't it?"

Rhona stared at Dusty questioningly but she couldn't stop the blush from deepening. She capitulated. "It was a long time ago. Before they were married."

"What happened?"

Rhona's interrogatory stare questioned the need for Dusty to know the answer to that question. Dusty persisted.

"I understand it may not be relevant to my investigation, but I need every possible piece of information about Blake. Only when I put all the pieces together, will I know what's important."

"I understand." Rhona's warm smile returned. "I knew you were the best. Being in the firing line myself wasn't what I was expecting though. You've dredged up something I'd almost forgotten and which I now find embarrassing." She placed a hand lightly on my arm as I made to move away, concerned my male presence might cause her further embarrassment. "It's all right. It's time I was adult enough to talk about it."

She glanced at the door. The group of women arriving highlighted the broad ethnic mix in Broome which I'd already noticed in the town since I arrived. Among them were two women in their early twenties; a fair haired Anglo Australian woman and a pregnant woman with a purple streak in her dark hair, I guessed to be of mixed Aboriginal Australian heritage. They ascended the stairs, possibly to take advantage of the shower and bathroom facilities. Two other women with Asian features went over to the servery area where Tavish stood behind an array of bains-marie with hot food.

Rhona took a deep breath and confessed to what she'd been reluctant to reveal. "Nothing happened between Blake and me. I would never do that to my sister. I did fancy him and, I'm ashamed to say, I flirted with him. I suppose it's a point in his favour that he ignored me. In a weird kind of way, his being loyal to Tiri made him even more attractive to me."

"Is that when you first turned against Blake? When he rejected you?"

"Yes. I hated him with the all-consuming passion of a fifteen-year-old. That's how old I was at the time. Nothing but a silly kid really."

I recalled Jack's comment about Rhona having some sort of long term grudge against Blake. Not idle gossip after all.

"Tiri must have noticed," said Dusty.

"She thought I was being a moody teenager. Besides, I didn't see them much. I was still living at home in Wales; they lived in London. Then a few months later, I met my first boyfriend so I had a new focus for my affections."

"You and Blake never became good friends?"

"Not good friends, but I stopped hating him. Teenagers can be like that; what seems to be imperative to their happiness one minute is yesterday's news the next. You could say Blake and I established friendly relations and we were polite to each other." The softness in her brown eyes was replaced with a steely look. "Until he murdered Tiri." Rhona gripped Dusty's arm. "That man mustn't be allowed to get away with murder again. He's rich, famous, handsome and charming which adds up to a lot of power. He uses his power to manipulate others, including the police."

Dusty raised her eyebrows. "You're not suggesting he bribed the police handling Tiri's case?"

"He wouldn't need to be that crass. He'd use his charm and, by implication, his fame and power."

A notification beep on Rhona's phone interrupted our conversation. After a glance at the screen she beamed at us. "It's Matilda." She got up and moved away to take the call.

I looked out the window. The tattooed man in the baseball cap was still leaning up against the tree. At this moment he was scratching his crotch in that posturing way some men have, signalling their dominance like a dog marking its territory.

I pointed him out to Dusty, wondering if he was waiting for one of the women in here.

"He's been there most of the morning like."

"Interesting." Dusty gazed thoughtfully through the window.

Rhona returned to the table. "That was Matilda on the phone. I mean, Inspector Matilda Lyons, the lead detective on the team that investigated Fern's murder. She'll help you in any way she can."

"Great. Is she a friend of yours?"

Rhona raised her eyebrows. "You don't know who she is?"

"Inspector Lyons? I don't think so." Dusty looked enquiringly at me. I shook my head.

"She tried to save my sister's life. She's Inspector Lyons now. She was Senior Constable Lyons seventeen years ago."

"Sounds familiar but…" A puzzled frown crossed Dusty's face. She paused and slapped the side of her head with the heel of her hand. "Senior Constable Lyons! She was the hero the night Tiri died, wasn't she?"

"Don't call her a hero; it's not a label she's comfortable with. She always says she was merely doing her job."

"I'd really like to talk to her."

"She suggested meeting you at Queen City Marina later in the week. I'll text you her number."

As we were leaving, I asked Rhona if she knew the tattooed man waiting across the street. After a glance the man, she shook her head.

"I don't think I've seen him before. Hopefully, he's not lurking with sinister intent toward one of the women."

"I'll have a word with him," said Dusty. "A friendly chat to suss him out." A concerned expression crossed Rhona's face. "Don't worry. I'll have my bodyguard with me." Dusty grinned and gestured at me. She has jokingly referred to me as her protector in the past but, as a karate black belt, Dusty has never needed me in that capacity.

When we left the air conditioned comfort of the drop-in centre, it took me a few minutes to adjust to the humidity outside. The tattooed man was still there, shielded from some of the heat by the shade of the tree. He was slouching with hands in pockets, his eyes hidden behind the mirrored lenses of his sunglasses. Dusty and I crossed the street and approached him casually.

# CHAPTER 8

M Y FIRST INDICATION things were not as they seemed, was the grin on Dusty's face when she drew close to the man.

"Hello, my clever friend," she said.

The man removed his sunglasses. That was the moment I recognised him. It wasn't a man at all. It was Jack.

She giggled, delighted to have caused the startled expression on my face. "Your jaw is dropping, Seamus."

When the two women had stopped laughing, Jack stood back with both arms out. "Did I pass the test?"

Dusty nodded emphatically. "Yep. Sean had no idea it was you. Everyone at Pearl's Shell thought you were a lurking man. Actually, I didn't know it was you at first." She turned to me. "I told you Jack had the power of invisibility. She uses different disguises so whoever she's tailing doesn't realise they're seeing the same person."

Jack put her sunglasses back on. "I might want to use this disguise again so I'll head in the opposite direction. We don't want people in Broome knowing I'm on your team." Still in character, she slouched away.

Dusty watched her for a moment with an affectionate smile then turned to me.

"When my Mum disappeared they tried to take me away."

This random statement caused me a moment of bewilderment before I realised she was referring to her earlier comment when we were at the children's play area.

"You mean social services?"

"Yes. According to them my Dad couldn't look after me on his own. They were going to take me away and place me in some sort of foster arrangement. Can you believe that?"

Dusty had never shared this with me before. "What happened?"

"It was about six months after Mum disappeared. One of the kids at school broke the news to me. She started chanting: *They're coming to get you. They're coming to get you.* I ran down to the end of the playground, climbed up into a big tree and cried my heart out. I was so petrified. I wouldn't get out of the tree."

It was not difficult to imagine five-year-old Dusty being stubborn enough to stay in the tree all day. I could also imagine how terrified she must have been at the thought of being taken away from the father she adored, especially in light of the recent loss of her mother.

"Eventually, Dad came and got me. After that, I clung to him all the time. I wouldn't let him leave to go to work. He had to take time off and stay at home all day until my Nan arrived. She moved in with us." Dusty's grandmother, whom she called Nan, became a second mother to her.

"Why did they think your father couldn't look after you properly?"

Dusty's nostrils flared. "I was being extremely well looked after. When Dad was at work I was with Uncle and Auntie and all my cousins." Although I didn't know Auntie, I had met Uncle; an Australian Aboriginal man who impressed me with his sagacity and insight. He and Dusty's father had worked together and were as close as brothers. Dusty used *Uncle* as a term of respect. He was not technically her uncle, but her godfather. "But that wasn't good enough for social services."

"Because you were with an Aboriginal family?"

I had learned enough about the history of Australia to know Aboriginal people had been viewed in the past as uncivilized because of their hunter gatherer lifestyle. Although their culture is better understood, respected and celebrated these days, the residual effect of the historical view probably still influenced the thinking of some people back in the 1980s. The idea of Dusty being part of her godfather's 'tribe' must have set alarm bells ringing. Any intelligent person who met Uncle would have realised he and his family provided the security blanket and love Dusty needed in the midst of uncertainty. However, prejudice can override intelligence to produce what my grandmother would call 'gormless eejits'.

"They didn't say that, but that's what I think." Outrage flashed in Dusty's eyes. As the anger subsided, her smile returned. "Anyway, the social services department has improved since then."

Across the street, two women were leaving Pearl's Shell. One of them was the woman with the purple stripe in her hair I'd noticed on the stairs earlier. The other one was Noelene. She hurried across the road to us.

"I had an idea this lady wanted to tell me something," said Dusty.

"So did I." Dusty expressed her approval of my powers of observation with a thumbs-up gesture.

Noelene joined us in the shade of the tree. "Can I talk to you?"

"Of course," said Dusty. "What's on your mind?"

"The thing is, I know you're here to investigate Fern Parkes's murder but…" Noelene glanced back at Pearl's Shell.

"It's all right, Noelene. The smallest bit of information can be helpful, even if it seems totally irrelevant. Sometimes it turns out to be important."

"It's about Petra."

"Petra?"

"She was murdered, too."

"A friend of yours?"

"Petra and I worked together. She was a good friend."

"I'm so sorry."

It wasn't unusual for people to approach Dusty asking for her help in solving the murder of a loved one. She always treated them with respect and sympathy but the reality was she had a long waiting list of cold cases. In general, Dusty didn't allow herself to be influenced by the emotions of others but she found it difficult to tell grieving relatives she was too busy to help them. Her anxious anticipation of such a request about to be made by Noelene showed in her expression. However, Noelene's next words surprised both of us.

"Within two weeks of Fern's murder, two other women were killed in the same spot."

"Serious? How awful." Dusty and I exchanged shocked glances.

Three women killed in the same place? Surely that can't be a coincidence. In a small town like Broome a group of women being murdered has to be a rare event. I wondered why it hadn't been a hot news item. On the other hand, I vaguely recalled reports of it in the Melbourne press. Now that I thought about it, I realised a car rampage in Bourke Street had happened around the same time. That shocking event would have overshadowed news of this tragedy far away in Western Australia.

"Was your friend one of the other victims?" asked Dusty.

"Yes. The second one." Noelene looked down at the ground for a moment. "The police think Petra and Vicki, the third victim, were killed by a copycat killer. So does Rhona."

That might explain why Rhona hadn't mentioned the other murders.

"You don't agree?" said Dusty.

"It seems a bit dubious, don't you think, two murderers in a town this size?"

Dusty studied Noelene's face before answering.

"I agree it seems unusual. However, it's not impossible. If the police have arrived at that conclusion they must have good reason for it."

Noelene's expression suggested she had little faith in the deductive powers of the police. "I think they're putting all their resources into proving Blake Montgomery murdered his wife instead of looking at the big picture."

"You think all three women were killed by the same person; a serial killer?"

Noelene shrugged. "Seems more likely to me than two murderers."

Dusty reassured her. "Sometimes murder investigations take months to resolve. The police need to have enough evidence to make an arrest before they can take action. I'm sure they're still working on your friend's case."

Noelene inclined her head in acknowledgement of Dusty's point. "You're right; I need to be more patient."

"Being impatient to see your friend's killer behind bars is perfectly natural. As time passes, it's normal for friends and relatives to start to worry that the murderer will never be caught."

Noelene smiled her appreciation at Dusty's understanding.

"I promise you, if I believe there's a connection to all three murders, I will investigate that angle."

"If there's anything I can do to help you with your investigation, just ask."

Dusty passed her phone, open at the contacts menu, to Noelene. "Would you mind adding your number?"

Noelene obliged, handed the phone back and added, "I'm really glad you're here, Ms Kent. The police don't seem to have a clue."

"Please call me Dusty."

Noelene hoisted her bag over her shoulder. "I'd best get off to the gym." She flashed us a parting smile before striding away.

"Interesting," said Dusty as we strolled back toward where the car was parked. "I wonder if Noelene has heard something, some local gossip perhaps, to make her think the three murders were committed by the same killer."

"She doesn't seem to be the sort of person to put much store by gossip."

"Exactly. That's why I'm curious. I hope she's not keeping a secret which could put her in danger."

"If she's right, if the women were killed by a serial killer," I said, "it's not going to be Blake Montgomery, is it?"

Dusty was not ready to let go of her prime suspect. "Unless he killed Fern in the heat of the moment then, when the police were getting too close, panicked and murdered two other women to make it look like a serial killer was on the loose."

Such a scenario seemed improbable to me but I knew Dusty liked to consider every possibility and 'leave no stone unturned'.

# CHAPTER 9

I HAD ASSUMED Inspector Lyons would be in police uniform for our meeting on Friday. However, she was waiting for us at Queen City Marina in a cream coloured dress and matching light jacket; a smart casual look, less intimidating than a uniform but not too informal. Leaning against the timber balustrade at the end of the retail promenade with a backdrop of yachts behind her, she was keeping a watchful eye on the tourists wandering along the cafe precinct, probably on the lookout for us.

I recognised her from a photo I'd found online when Dusty asked me to 'do some digging'. After our meeting with Rhona earlier in the week, Dusty had wondered how the police launch had been on the scene so quickly the night Tiri Welsh fell overboard. I discovered Blake and Tiri's yacht, *Tooting Moon*, had been under police surveillance as a possible transporter of drugs.

"Drugs! I knew it." Dusty was triumphant. "What else did you find out?"

The police had been suspicious when *Tooting Moon* made several trips to a remote atoll on the Western Australian coast at a time when the state was experiencing a methamphetamine crisis. Frustrated that the Federal agencies were not putting enough effort into stopping the trade, the Western Australian Police were doing their best to control the drug smuggling.

Senior Sergeant Mark Thorn had suspected Blake was a courier, picking up drugs which had been dropped off at Rowley Shoals. He decided to keep a close eye on *Tooting Moon*, especially at night. Consequently, he and his colleague Senior Constable Lyons were not far from the yacht, hidden from view in the dark with their lights off, when they received the SOS call. They swung into action with Thorn at the helm and Lyons scanning the ocean with the aid of the vessel's search light.

When Senior Constable Lyons caught a glimpse of a red sarong floating in the water, she'd removed her outer clothing and dived in, almost before the vessel had stopped. Unfortunately, she hadn't been able to locate Tiri Welsh at first. By the time she found Tiri's body and got her back onto the police launch with the help of her colleague, it was too late. Even the pair's desperate attempts to revive Tiri were in vain.

Senior Constable Lyons's courageous actions in trying to save the life of Tiri Welsh were broadcast around the world. She was awarded a medal of valour.

"It was an awesome thing to do," said Dusty. "I wouldn't fancy diving into an ocean at night looking for a drowning woman."

Dusty attracted the attention of Inspector Lyons with a wave.

"Please call me Matilda," said the police inspector when she introduced herself. "Welcome to beautiful Broome. For me it's welcome back. I'm based in Perth these days."

Her occupation was reflected in the sternly etched fine lines on a face sprinkled with freckles and devoid of make-up. She wore her brown hair drawn up into a smooth bun. A welcoming smile took years off her appearance. I changed my initial assessment of her age from mid forties to late thirties.

I looked for traces of the young Senior Constable Lyons whose photo I had seen on the internet but the years, or her occupation, had erased the eager blush of youth. However, I fancied I saw traces of the hero who dived into the ocean. I sensed she was still committed to doing her duty, to saving lives and helping people.

Inspector Lyons gestured at the water beyond the marina. "It's a shame we're here to discuss murder, isn't it?"

Dusty agreed. "It does seem incongruous. That the murders happened here on the marina is even more discordant. All the yachts, the boardwalks and the cafe precinct create a convivial atmosphere." She indicated the area with a sweep of her arm and added, "Thanks for taking time out to help me with this investigation."

"Rhona was very persuasive." Inspector Lyons smiled. "Besides, your reputation goes before you."

"Thank you, Matilda. I'll make a point of passing on anything relevant. Naturally, you and your team will be given full credit for their hard work in the book I write documenting my investigation."

This was Dusty's usual way of repaying the police for their co-operation. The media would focus on the police who made the arrest. Dusty's reward was the opportunity to write another bestselling book.

Inspector Lyons understood. "I've read your books; I know you give credit where credit is due."

"When I've got the killer in my sights, I'll let you know so your team can make the arrest."

If the Inspector was disconcerted by Dusty's brash self confidence, she didn't allow it to show.

"That sounds fair. If you can turn up something new, we'd be grateful." The Inspector reached into the document bag she carried with her and drew out several files. "These are copies of the case notes." She handed them to Dusty. "I can get you access to the full files if you would like to see them. I'll need to clear it with my superiors but I don't think there'll be a problem."

"This'll be enough to get me started." Dusty placed the files in her shoulder bag which seemed to have a bottomless capacity. "Do you think Rhona is right in assuming Blake Montgomery killed Fern?"

Inspector Lyons hesitated. When she answered she chose her words carefully. "In all likelihood, Mr Montgomery killed his first wife by pushing her into the ocean. It suggests he has a ruthless streak. For that reason, he cannot be ignored as a suspect in the murder of his second wife. Furthermore, he doesn't have an alibi for the time of her death."

"But?"

"We found no evidence linking him to Fern Parkes's murder." She gestured at the timber boardwalk running along the water's edge where the yachts were moored. "This will take us to the alleyway where Ms Parkes was murdered."

A cool breeze off the ocean diluted some of the heat of the morning as we walked three abreast past the rows of yachts with water lapping around their hulls.

Inspector Lyons pointed to the other side of the boardwalk where an old sailing ship was anchored. "It's a replica of the Ida Lloyd, a wooden pearl lugger lost at sea in 2007 after breaking free of its moorings. This one's a museum ship permanently moored here; a drawcard for tourists. Before they board the Ida Lloyd, visitors walk through a display area where they can watch an old black and white film featuring an interview with an actual pearler. Diving costumes and steel helmets that were once used are also on display." The Inspector resumed walking. "I lived in Broome when I first joined WAPOL."

Dusty's brows furrowed. "WAPOL?"

"Western Australia Police." Inspector Lyons smiled and continued. "It was partly because of my local knowledge that I was sent back here to head up the investigation when Fern Parkes was murdered."

Dusty's eyebrows furrowed. "Was that difficult – treating Blake Montgomery as a suspect in his second wife's murder? I mean, you must have formed some sort of connection with him after what happened when his first wife died." Perhaps mindful of Rhona's comment about the Inspector being a reluctant hero, Dusty refrained from mentioning her role in trying to save the life of Tiri Welsh.

"I didn't have any problems with that aspect. It's not as if we were friends or anything. I didn't have much to do with Mr Montgomery back then. I was not part of the investigation into Tiri Welsh's death. He wrote to me after he returned to the United States thanking me for what I did but that was it."

"What was the police chat at the time? Did the investigators have a strong sense of what really happened the night Tiri died?"

"The general consensus was that Blake Montgomery had pushed his wife over the edge of the yacht during a heated argument, either without heed for her safety or with the intention of killing her. It was hearsay; not fact. All we know for sure is Tiri Welsh died in the ocean that night. How she ended up in the water is a mystery that will probably never be solved. Unfortunately, there's just as much mystery about how Montgomery's second wife died." Inspector Lyons paused at the entrance to an uncovered walkway fenced on both sides with thick nautical style rope looped between evenly spaced pier piles. "This is the new pedestrian walkway. The murders were committed in the old one, which is more of an alley." The Inspector pointed ahead. "It's up there."

"You said 'murders'. I understand two other women were murdered the same month in the same spot?"

The cautious police inspector glanced around to make sure no-one was within earshot before answering. "Correct. Ms Parkes was the first of three women killed in the alley. Did Rhona tell you?"

"She didn't. We heard it from someone else. Why didn't she tell me?"

"She doesn't accept the possibility the deaths could be linked. Rhona's concerned that police could put the three murders down to a serial killer."

"And that would rule out Blake Montgomery?"

"Correct. Although connecting the three homicides doesn't necessarily rule him out."

The Inspector's statement caused Dusty to slow her step. "You think he might have killed three women?"

"I'm not suggesting that. However, it is possible the other two murders were copycat killings. If we can prove that, the possibility Montgomery killed his wife remains."

"Copycat? You mean he kills to copy someone else and no other reason?"

"Correct. He wants to get the same notoriety. Fern Parkes was once a Hollywood actor and was married to a famous Hollywood star whose first wife died in mysterious circumstances right here in this area. Naturally, her murder attracted a lot of media coverage. A common motivation for copycat killers is the desire to get the same sort of attention as the murderer they are emulating."

Dusty shook her head. "It makes me sick to think someone could be that depraved."

The thought of anyone killing another human being just to get attention created a knot in my stomach. Murder was evil enough but copycat killing was seriously sick.

"We think he killed the second victim hoping to get similar media coverage as the first murder received. That didn't happen. The media was still preoccupied with Fern Parkes."

"So it's possible he killed the third victim because the second murder didn't have the impact he wanted."

"That's precisely what we believe."

We were interrupted by a male voice behind us. "Inspector Lyons." I immediately recognised a posh English accent, the sort BBC newsreaders used to have.

# CHAPTER 10

We all turned around. Walking toward us waving a hand in greeting was a man in his late fifties wearing tan deck shoes, a pair of knee length shorts, a short-sleeved blue shirt, and dark sunglasses.

When he drew level with us, he extended his hand to the Inspector. The Rolex watch on his wrist caught my attention. Posh English accent. Posh watch. Both seemed out of place in Broome. Inspector Lyons accepted the handshake with a polite smile. The man's face seemed familiar. It wasn't until he pushed his sunglasses to the top of his head that I recognised him. He turned to shake hands with Dusty, his charming smile revealing excellent teeth.

"You must be Dusty Kent."

"Please call me Dusty. You must be Blake Montgomery."

"Please call me Blake." He grinned.

"This is my assistant, Sean O'Kelly."

I resisted the temptation to say 'Please call me Sean'.

Blake turned to the Inspector. "I was on my way to the boat when I spotted you." He directed his attention back to Dusty. "Inspector Lyons and I chanced to meet the other day. She mentioned you were coming to Broome to investigate what happened to my wife." The grin had faded.

"I was planning on bringing Dusty to the yacht later, Mr Montgomery. She would like to interview you."

At first the formality between Blake and Inspector Lyons seemed incongruous then I realised he was a suspect in a case the police were still working on. I sensed it was the Inspector who made sure the convention was maintained.

"Of course." The broad smile Blake offered Inspector Lyons was one that would undoubtedly melt the resistance of a less flinty recipient. "I'm happy to help in any way I can if it means getting the lowlife who murdered Fern." His face darkened but cleared when he gestured toward the ocean. "Y'know, I'm taking the boat out on the water later. You're all welcome to come along. We can catch the high tide just before lunch."

The Inspector declined the offer but Dusty and I arranged to meet Blake at the *Doris* when we had finished our business with Inspector Lyons.

As he walked away, Dusty looked after him thoughtfully. A man as charming as Blake Montgomery was sure to make her suspicious.

"So that's the famous Hollywood star in the flesh," she said. "I didn't expect him to have a British accent. I've only ever heard him speaking with an American accent in movies."

"He was born in England," said Inspector Lyons. "I can probably tell you everything you want to know about Blake Montgomery. On second thoughts, I'm not sure if that's true. I wonder if he has a few secrets our investigation hasn't unearthed." She pointed ahead. "The old alleyway is up there. It's now known locally as Murder Alley."

As we walked on, Dusty returned to the earlier conversation.

"Matilda, before we were interrupted, you mentioned the possibility of a copycat killer. Why copycat? Why not a serial killer? Could the same person have killed all three women?"

"We did consider that. As a matter of fact, a local ABC news presenter received a note from someone claiming to be the killer. He said he murdered all three women and would kill again. Our forensic team reached the conclusion the second two murders were most likely the work of a copycat killer."

"You mean you thought the letter was a hoax?"

"Not a hoax. A frangipani was enclosed with the letter. Only the killer would have known a single frangipani bloom was placed in the hair of the second and third victims. You know the flowers I mean, white with a yellow centre. Women sometimes wear them in their hair as decoration."

"This guy is seriously depraved." Dusty grimaced in disgust.

"Apart from the murderer, no one outside our investigative team knew about the flower."

"So you believe the note was sent by the murderer, but you weren't convinced he'd killed all three women?"

"Correct. Rather than a message from a serial killer, we believe it was from a copycat frustrated at not getting enough attention who wanted to share the notoriety associated with the murder of Fern Parkes."

We had arrived at the entrance to Murder Alley. A sign directed people to use the new walkway but the alley was not closed off.

Inspector Lyons pointed to the far end of the boardwalk.

"Two of the victims had been to Diamond Box; a cocktail bar down there."

Dusty peered along the boardwalk at the stylish white building in the distance. The design of the bar was reminiscent of a luxury yacht with windows all around to take advantage of the view over the water. "Doesn't look like a box. Or a diamond."

"Or a diamond box," I added.

"It's named after the famous box of diamonds which went missing in 1942."

"Sounds like an intriguing story." Dusty was always interested in a mystery.

Inspector Lyons smiled. "It is. The diamonds in the box belonged to the Dutch government in Indonesia. They were worth millions of dollars. The box was put on a plane to be handed over to the Commonwealth Bank in Australia. Unfortunately, the plane arrived on March 3rd, 1942; the same day Japanese fighter planes attacked Broome."

"Oh, no!" Dusty's hand flew to her chest. "A lot of people were killed during that attack, weren't they?"

"At least eighty-eight people, maybe more."

"And the plane carrying the diamonds?" I was curious how a box of diamonds could disappear.

"The plane landed north of Broome after being shot down. Some of the passengers, Dutch evacuees from Java, were killed. The mail, which included the box of diamonds, was lost in the water."

The Inspector turned and pointed toward the cafe precinct at the opposite end of the marina boardwalk. "Anyone coming from Diamond Box can use this alley, or the new walkway, as a short cut to the retail precinct. From there you can get through to the car park. That's what the second victim was doing. She was on her way to the marina car park at 11.00pm after working a casual shift at the cocktail bar."

"You're talking about Petra Venter?"

"Yes. Thirty years old. Originally from South Africa. She was murdered nine days after Fern."

During our walk I had noticed the lack of surveillance cameras along the marina.

"There's no CCTV anywhere on the marina or the walkways," said Inspector Lyons when I asked her about it. "The only place you'll find security cameras is over in the retail section." She gestured at Murder Alley. "Fern Parkes was killed about halfway along the alleyway which is approximately six hundred metres long. Come; I'll show you."

# CHAPTER 11

"Was there anything other than the frangipanis to link the second and third murders to the same killer?" asked Dusty as we entered the alley.

Inspector Lyons acknowledged Dusty's need for clarification with a nod. "Yes. For example, all three women were hit over the head before being strangled, but the weapon used on Fern Parkes was not the same as that used on the other two victims."

"I see. You think a serial killer would stick with what had been successful the first time and used the same weapon to stun all his or her victims. What did he use on Fern?"

"Forensics believe it was a sock weapon."

"Serious? A sock?"

The Inspector explained. "A long sock with something heavy in the toe."

"Seems a bit primitive," said Dusty. "If you want to stun the victim first to avoid having to struggle with her, why not use a taser?"

This brought a stern look from Inspector Lyons. "Tasers are illegal. They're not available for sale in Australia. It would have been risky for the killer to buy one from an overseas online supplier because the purchase could be traced."

The alley was beginning to make me feel uncomfortable. We were following in the footsteps of three women who had been brutally murdered. At the same time as I had that thought I heard footsteps behind us, slow deliberate steps of one person. I turned my head. The alley was empty. The two women beside me, engrossed in their conversation, didn't appear to have noticed anything.

"Fair enough," said Dusty. "What sort of weapon was used on the other two victims?"

"A golf club."

Dusty reflected on this for a moment. "The use of different weapons doesn't necessarily rule out a serial killer. After using the sock weapon the first time, he might have realised he needed something that suited his purpose better. So he decided to change weapons."

"That is a possibility," conceded the Inspector. "However, something else was different about the first murder."

"No frangipani in Fern's hair," suggested Dusty.

"That's not all. The ligature used on her was different from the one used on the other two victims; a belt with distinctive markings."

"A belt?"

"What looks like a belt. Possibly a man's belt. Star shaped perforations along the edges left the same unique imprint on the skin of both victims."

"You didn't find the same imprint on Fern's neck?"

Inspector Lyons shook her head firmly. "If a belt was used on Fern, it was a different kind of belt. I'm inclined to think it was a cord of some sort. Another factor we considered was that the killing stopped." The triumphant gleam in the Inspector's eye suggested she had saved her strongest point for last.

"You think a copycat killer was more likely to stop than a serial killer?"

"A serial murderer usually keeps killing for the thrill he gets from it. If he'd already gotten away with killing three women, why would he stop? The motivation of a copycat killer is different. The second two murders did not get the same media attention as Fern's. That was partly because the victims were not well-known identities but also because we asked the press to keep the reporting of the other two murders as low key as possible. We realised we might have a copycat on our hands and wanted to stop him by making sure he didn't get the buzz of media notoriety."

"He gave up because he didn't get the attention he'd anticipated?"

"Correct. Also the police presence in Broome at the time was strong. We concluded he decided it was too much risk for not enough reward."

"Makes sense – in a macabre kind of way."

I remained alert for footsteps behind us but heard nothing. Strangely, this was even more unsettling. I had a sense of someone following us with a soundless tread. It took an effort for me to maintain my concentration on the discussion.

"So the police investigation is treating Fern's murder as separate from the other two," continued Dusty.

"Correct."

"You said you found no evidence to suggest her husband was the killer. Did you find any evidence pointing to someone else?"

"We did consider another suspect. However, we found no evidence he had reason to harm Fern and nothing to link him to the murder."

"Who?"

"Fern's lover. It's possible she broke off their relationship that night. She may have been on her way back to her yacht when she was killed, not on her way to meet him. He might have been enraged at her rejection and threatened her. She fled from him. He followed her and killed her in the alley."

"You mean he crept up behind her, knocked her over the head then took off his belt and strangled her?"

"That scenario is entirely possible."

"Why would he choose to finish the job with strangulation? If he was in a rage, wouldn't he have hit her over the head until she was dead?"

"It's possible he panicked after he attacked her. At this point, he's not in the same heightened state of fury but he realises he'll need to kill her. He looks down at her beautiful face and can't bring himself to disfigure it with further blows so decides to strangle her instead."

"Strangulation doesn't necessarily leave the victim's face looking pretty, does it?"

"No. But he might not have known that."

"I take it you didn't find a belt or a cord with incriminating DNA on it in his possession?"

"We did not. But you'd expect him to get rid of it. The same goes for Mr Montgomery. We searched his yacht thoroughly and carried out forensic tests on his belts and socks and found nothing."

"What about a golf club? You said the other two women were stunned with a blow from a golf club. Did Blake have one on board the yacht?"

"We weren't looking for such an item when we searched his yacht. Mr Montgomery has never been under investigation for the other two murders."

The look Dusty gave me suggested she thought the police should have been more thorough. We continued walking. If we were still being followed, our stalker was skilled in the art of stealth.

Murder Alley was wide enough for four or five people to walk abreast. It was not enclosed except for a wooden wall approximately two metres high running along the outer side for the length of the ablution buildings. The wall provided privacy for those using the amenities but also allowed concealment for a murderer.

"This ablutions block was closed down a couple of years ago when new amenities were built at the end of the cafe precinct. Then the new walkway was built, the one we passed earlier. This one has been earmarked for demolition."

The entrances to the toilets and showers were blocked by padlocked wire gates. Inspector Lyons paused in front of one of the locked gates.

"This was the shower section. Inside, it separates with women on the left and men on the right."

She advanced a few paces past the gates and pointed to the ground. "This is where Fern's body was found, as well as the bodies of the other two victims."

Dusty looked around and walked back a few paces. "The killer might have hidden himself here." She pointed to an alcove created by the shower gate being set back from the wall edge.

"Correct," said the Inspector. "It's the only place he could have hidden. The gates to both toilets are level with the wall so there's no recess there."

"If he's waiting here, and she's coming from this direction like we just did, she wouldn't see him. Check it out, Sean." Dusty slipped into the side corner of the recess. I hurried back a few paces. Before I turned around to walk toward the recess, I scanned the alley for the stalker but saw no-one.

As I passed the padlocked entrance, Dusty jumped out of the recess. "Did you see me in your peripheral vision as you approached?"

"No. Not at all."

"Also, it would be dim in here at night," said Inspector Lyons. "The only lights in operation are the ones at either end."

"Why did the women use this alley instead of taking the new walkway?" I asked.

"They were all locals and would have been in the habit of using it before the new one was built. In the case of the second two victims coming from Diamond Box, this is the first walkway they came to."

"I can understand why Fern chose to use this alleyway," I said. "She wanted to keep a low profile to reduce the risk of being recognised while on her way to her lover. But why did the other two women use it? Wouldn't they change their habits, knowing a murderer had been on the loose here?"

"Was the new walkway temporarily blocked off for construction work?" said Dusty.

"Nothing like that," said the Inspector. "I take your point. You would expect anyone walking along here at that time to steer well clear of the alley at night. Unfortunately, people don't always behave logically."

"True," agreed Dusty. "Matilda, I get the impression you see Fern's lover…" She broke off. "Who was her lover?"

"Wasim Smith; a personal trainer at Fern Parkes's wellness centre."

"I get the impression you see Wasim Smith as a more probable suspect than Blake Montgomery."

"Smith's alibi didn't check out; a red flag for me." Dusty and I fell in line with the Inspector as she began to stroll toward the exit. "He claims he was on the boardwalk outside his friend's yacht waiting for

Fern and spent the time until around midnight talking to a passing stranger. We did everything we could to track down the person he said he was with, using the description he gave us. We weren't able to find anyone who remembered seeing him."

"Giving a false alibi that can't be verified doesn't seem very smart."

"It's possible nervousness during the police interview caused him to blurt out what he thought was a good alibi. Once he'd done that, he was compelled to stick to it or admit to lying."

Lying to the police must indicate Smith had something to hide. It was starting to look like Rhona's assumption that Montgomery had killed his wife might be wrong.

As we continued toward the alley exit leading to the retail precinct, I heard the footsteps behind us again; a furtive, ghostly tread. This time I determined to face our stalker, and my fears. I turned sharply. The alley behind us was deserted.

"Something wrong?" asked Inspector Lyons.

"Um." Should I keep my mouth shut? "Nothing wrong." Both women were looking at me, waiting for an answer. "I thought I heard footsteps behind us, that's all."

The Inspector suppressed a smile. "When people walk along the new walkway, for some reason, their footsteps can sometimes be heard in here."

I breathed a sigh of relief. "I knew that!"

The women laughed.

As we left the alley, the Inspector checked the time on her phone. "Mr Montgomery should be about ready to take the yacht out. I have to get back to work for a meeting, but if there's anything else you need, please get in touch."

"So," said Dusty, after Inspector Lyons left, "we have a possible new suspect. Wasim Smith. But if he isn't the killer," she looked at me with a gleam of mischief in her eyes, "you and I are about to spend the day out in the middle of the ocean with a murderer."

I wish she hadn't said that.

# CHAPTER 12

"CLIMB ABOARD." BLAKE hailed us from the deck when we arrived at the *Doris*; a shimmering white 52-foot motor yacht, probably custom built.

Once on board, Blake grinned at us playfully. "I omitted to tell you you're down for crew duty today. I'll get you to pull the slip lines while I take the helm. Think you can manage it?"

Dusty shrugged. "How hard can it be?" As far as I knew Dusty's experience with sailing was limited to helping out on fishing dinghies and speed boats during her childhood in East Gippsland. However, it was typical of her to meet a challenge with an optimistic 'can do' attitude.

"With this yacht it couldn't be easier," said Blake. "First thing is to remove your shoes while on board."

He showed us where to store our footwear. As peak caps were available for sun protection, I decided to remove my hat as well as my shoes; the wind at sea could be just as capricious as a sly camel.

"Put these on." Blake handed each of us a two way radio head set. "It'll make things a lot easier if we can talk to each other. I'm going to be in the wheel house so I won't be able to see you at all times but if we all wear these things we can communicate. One of your responsibilities as crew will be to let me know if I'm in danger of steering into anything as we pull away. Your other job is to take the slip ropes off." Blake explained what we needed to do with the slip ropes before heading up to the wheel house. "You're lucky you won't have to pull fenders up."

"Fenders?" Dusty and I exchanged the confused looks of the uninitiated. My sailing experience was as inadequate as Dusty's. Growing up in Roscommon in north-central Ireland gave me little opportunity to get acquainted with seafaring vessels. I had joined the crew of a fishing trawler along the west coast of Australia since arriving in this country but that was hardly similar to a luxury yacht.

"Fenders are like cushions that hang over the side to protect the boat from knocking against the dock. They can be a trifle heavy. I've got permanent dock bumpers here so we don't need them."

"What a shame. Sean could have got a good workout."

Blake acknowledged Dusty's joke with a broad grin.

"It won't take long to get underway," he said as he disappeared inside.

"How good is this?" Dusty was enjoying her role as deckhand. We managed to complete our tasks without mishap and receive the thumbs-up from our captain as the yacht drew away from the marina. He beckoned us to join him up in the wheel house.

"Keep a look out for golf clubs." Dusty whispered as we made our way single file up the narrow stairway. "And we need to get into his cabin."

"His cabin? What on earth for?" Following her example, I kept my voice low. Dusty turned back to me and whispered. "A belt with a star-shaped pattern along the edges. A diary confessing his guilt. A hiding place for drugs. Anything that might turn out to be incriminating evidence." I could have reminded her my skills lay in cyber space not real life espionage. Risking my life by spying on a potential serial killer wasn't something I'd signed up for. However, I had no time to object as we'd already reached the top of the steps.

Blake turned away from the helm as we entered to greet us with a broad smile. "Welcome to the cockpit of fabulous *Doris*."

The wheel house was awe inspiring. Windows all around at eye level gave Blake an almost 360 degree view of the ocean.

"Savage!" I couldn't hide my admiration.

Blake grinned. "Some boat, isn't she?"

"She's beautiful," said Dusty. "I'm curious about her name though."

Blake was enjoying our appreciation of his yacht and seemed

pleased at Dusty's question. "Y'know, most people don't bother to ask. They assume the boat's named after a woman."

"Doris Day?" Dusty was unable to keep the smirk from her face as she glanced at me.

"A common misconception," agreed Blake. "One of the tabloids in Los Angeles once ran an article on *Doris*, without any input from me. They were brazen in their lies, making statements like: *Mr Montgomery's deep respect for movie idol Doris Day is reflected in the name of his yacht.*" He shook his head. "Before you know it, the world accepts their trash as gospel truth."

I had no doubt his comment referred to something more than the reason for naming his yacht.

"The truth is, I named the yacht after a Greek sea nymph who ruled the oceans. Doris was a Goddess and mother of all the Nereids, as they are called. Sea nymphs are helpful to sailors." He paused. "Allegedly." A broad smile accompanied his next statement. "Either way, I decided it might be wise to pay homage to Doris in the hope she would keep the yacht safe and all who sail in her." A sombre expression passed across his face as he uttered the last words. Was he thinking of his first yacht and his first wife?

Noticing I had difficulty keeping my eyes off the dazzling display of instrument panels fitted along the wall underneath the window area, Blake offered to explain it all to me.

He pointed to a screen, smaller than the others, with a large round knob on one side. "This is the primary auto pilot. I couldn't take the boat out on my own without it." He gestured to a duplicate screen underneath. "This is the back-up auto pilot in case the first one fails."

It didn't take long before the yacht was cruising in the open sea. Blake adjusted the knob on the primary auto pilot. "Now I'm free."

When he began to explain the function of the various display screens and panels, Dusty saw her opportunity.

"I'll duck down to the ladies room."

"It's the heads you're after, young lady." Blake grinned at Dusty. "I'll show you where they are."

Dusty raised her palm in the stop sign gesture. "Absolutely not.

No need to tear you two away from your boys' toys. Point me in the right direction. I'll find my own way."

Blake acquiesced and told Dusty where to find 'the heads'. I doubted that was where Dusty really wanted to go. She would take this opportunity to search the yacht for evidence. My job was to keep the skipper occupied for as long as possible.

Blake started his tour of the display area with a screen that seemed to consist of several rows of digital and analogue tachometer style gauges.

"This system is my right hand man," he said, his broad smile revealing his enjoyment of his 'toys'. "It allows me to keep an eye on what is going on with almost every instrument in the boat. As long as I see only green lights on this panel, I know everything is fine."

"And if there's a red light?"

"A red light alerts me to something wrong and tells me exactly where the problem is."

I was soon lost in a fascinating tour of the electronic displays of maps and instrument panels in the cockpit. Distracting Blake took no effort on my part. He obviously relished the opportunity to explain the workings of the yacht to a captive audience. His pride was evident in his shining eyes as he gave me a tour of all the navigational display screens and instrument panels which included a multi-voltage power system, on-screen maps, multi-function displays, engine control displays and more.

It was hard to imagine this man as a wife-killer. And yet, I knew enough about murderers to realise his charming demeanour might be the very reason he could be the controlling, abusive type of spouse capable of violence. He might be what Dusty called a narcissistic personality capable of hiding behind a socially acceptable facade. Furthermore, he was an accomplished actor. A flash of dread surged through me when I realised what a dangerous combination that was.

"I wonder where the lovely Dusty has got to," he said when he'd finished the tour of the cockpit.

"Oh, she's probably staying out of the way." I hoped I'd managed to make that sound like an offhand remark. "I'm afraid she'd find all this awesome technical stuff boring."

Blake laughed. "Let's go tell her it's safe to return."

Before I could think of what to say to stop him, he'd left the wheel house and was clambering down the steps. I had visions of Dusty engrossed in a search of Blake's wardrobe, inspecting his belts unaware of him entering the cabin. I hastened after him, speaking as loudly as I could without being too obvious.

"Dusty might be taking in the ocean views on a deck somewhere. Dusty loves the ocean." I repeated her name in the hope it would make its way into her consciousness wherever she was.

The galley was empty. My eyes went toward the master bedroom off the galley. Was Dusty in there searching through Blake's things?

I called out to her. "Dusty!"

"While we're here," said Blake, "come and take a look at the navigational system in my cabin. Those displays in the wheel house are repeated down here so I can keep an eye on things from my bed."

How could I prevent him from going in there? His hand was on the doorknob. Dusty was about to be caught red-handed. My brain was scrambling. To my relief, Dusty appeared from around a corner.

"Looking for me?" Her cheerful smile and casual attitude seemed perfectly natural. "I couldn't resist going outside to feel the sea spray on my face."

"Ah," said Blake. "If I'd known, I would have insisted you wore a safety vest."

"It was a spur of the moment thing. Anyway, there's not much wind."

Blake shook his head in gentle admonishment. "Wind conditions can change before you realise it."

Dusty looked contrite. We decided to return to the cockpit to, as Blake put it, 'get the business you need to discuss over and done with'. We turned around and ascended the steps to the pilot house. With me leading the way, followed by Blake, I had no chance to talk to Dusty to find out whether her clandestine search had been successful.

Back in the wheel house, Blake gestured to the spacious lounge area behind the helm, which offered easy views of the marine world outside. I realised the skipper of the boat did in fact have a 360 degree view if he turned around and looked through the windows lining the walls of the lounge area. Gazing out at the expanse of ocean and blue skies yielded me a fleeting insight into the sense of freedom and peace living on such a yacht would offer. A lifestyle easily accessed in my imagination, but way beyond my means.

"Make yourselves comfortable." Blake indicated the padded bench seats around a large wooden table. I noticed, for the first time, how quiet it was inside the cockpit.

"This shouldn't take long," said Dusty once we were seated. "I only have a few questions."

"Shoot." Blake sat across from Dusty, his hands on the table in front of him, fingers interlocked. His position allowed him to see the instrument panels. So far Dusty had given no indication suggesting she'd found something useful during her spying excursion. I risked a glance at her now. She responded with an almost imperceptible shake of her head as she directed her attention to Blake.

"You know Rhona has asked me to investigate Fern's murder?"

Blake sighed. "Not to put too fine a point on it, she thinks I killed Fern. Nothing could be further from the truth. She arrived at that ludicrous conclusion because of her long held belief that I murdered her sister." A rueful smile crossed his face. "More than anything, and for Fern's sake, I want you to find her killer. But it won't change Rhona's viewpoint."

"If you don't mind," said Dusty, "I'd like to start with Tiri's death. What happened the night your first wife died?"

Blake spread his hands palms down on the table. "I'm sure you've read the newspaper reports. Most of them are inaccurate and speculative."

"I understand. Please tell me your side of the story." Blake glowered at Dusty's use of the word *story*. She raised a hand in apology. "By story I mean an account of what happened."

The scowl morphed into a self-deprecating grimace. He raised his hands and spread them apart. "Stupid of me to react like that. With most of the newspapers and much of the public assuming I lied about what happened that night, I think I've grown over sensitive."

He peered out at the ocean where sea swells were rising and falling. After a few moments he seemed to brace himself to recount the events of that tragic evening on another yacht seventeen years before.

# CHAPTER 13

BLAKE MONTGOMERY SPOKE softly, a nostalgic expression on his face, his fingers interlocked again.

"We were doing an overnight trip to Rowley Shoals; a favourite place of ours. It's remote; pristine. The water is warm. We'd stay a few days, snorkelling, walking along the beach, totally relaxing. Western Australia has one of the most sensational coastlines I've ever seen. Tiri and I both loved sailing along it and stopping off at various places." He cast a brief glance at the instrument panels before continuing. "It should have been a romantic evening on *Tooting Moon*. We had a few glasses of wine with the fabulous meal Tiri cooked. Then somehow we started yelling at each other."

"What was the fight about?"

"Jealousy."

That surprised me. I had expected him to deny, or at least play down, the role his jealous outbursts might have had in Tiri's death. His next words took me aback.

"Tiri was bristling with jealousy. She accused me of having an affair."

Dusty's head jerked to one side. She wasn't ready to believe this version of the cause of the argument. Blake sighed as though he'd expected her to react that way, as if he was used to people not believing him. However, he remained calm.

"Y'know, Tiri was always insanely jealous of my leading ladies." His tone was one of a patient parent explaining a truth to a disbelieving teenage daughter.

"I don't remember reading that in the newspaper reports." Dusty's sceptical tone suggested 'the teenage daughter' wasn't ready to accept the message.

A bitter smile crossed Blake's face. "No. They only reported what suited their purposes."

Dusty nodded her understanding. As a journalist she was aware of the tendency for media outlets to exaggerate and even falsify aspects of a situation in order to increase their audience.

"I see." This was the sombre tone of a teenage daughter who has accepted her illusions might not be reality. "Would you mind telling me how Tiri ended up in the water that night?" Dusty now appeared to be viewing Blake less like a suspect and more like a bereaved husband.

He acknowledged her attitude shift with an appreciative glance. After a few moments' reflection he began to recount the events of the evening of Tiri's death.

"We were sitting out on the deck after our meal. Tiri was looking exceptionally beautiful in a red sarong. It was a perfect evening until I made the stupid mistake of suggesting we should invite some friends next time we did the trip."

"Tiri didn't like the idea?"

"She didn't object to inviting friends along. The problem was my mentioning a few of the friends by name, including the beautiful lady who was starring with me in the film I was working on at the time." He added with a self deprecating smile, "In retrospect, I could see how it appeared to Tiri. Here we were, hand in hand, enjoying being together and, in her eyes, my thoughts had wandered to another woman."

"Exactly!" Dusty was firmly in support of Tiri.

Having seven sisters has given me some insight into the workings of the female mind. I could understand how Tiri might have taken offence. From a male perspective I could also see the unreasonableness of her reaction. I decided to keep my mouth shut on that point.

"At the time, however, I was affronted to think she'd taken a straightforward suggestion and turned it into some sort of deviousness on my part." Blake's rueful smile affirmed his mistake. "I got angry because I believed she was being unreasonable. Then she got angry because she thought *I* was being unreasonable. In the end, she stormed back to our cabin. I allowed her a few moments to calm down before following her. Another rookie mistake." He rolled his eyes in recognition of his inexperience. "Apparently, if I cared about her I would have gone after her straight away."

Blake saw the condemnation in Dusty's eyes. He turned to me, an appeal for male understanding in his raised eyebrows. I tried to keep my expression non-committal, but he might have caught a hint of sympathy there as he continued.

"When I arrived at our cabin, Tiri erupted in another fit of temper about me not caring for her anymore. I tried to reason with her but she was too angry and upset to listen. In the end, she stomped out of the cabin." He blew out a deep breath. "I never saw her again."

Dusty leaned forward, a familiar gleam in her green eyes.

"Are you saying you were still in your cabin when Tiri went into the water?"

Blake lowered his eyes and nodded. Whether he knew it or not, he'd chosen a good way to evade the Dusty Kent Lie Detector. Dusty can almost always tell whether someone is lying by changes in their voice – especially when responding to a question. If the witness doesn't speak, she's unable to do that. Determined to get an answer, she tried again.

"Blake, did you see Tiri go overboard?"

"Y'know, Dusty, I thought you were meant to be focusing on Fern's murder." Blake got up and went over to the instrument panels, scrutinising each one.

"The audio alarms warn me if anything is amiss," he said, his back to us. "But I like to keep my eye on what is happening."

Did he change the subject because the trauma of speaking about Tiri's death was too much for him? Or did he want to avoid saying anything further in case he incriminated himself? Dusty exchanged a sceptical glance with me. I could see she suspected Blake of trying to avoid her scrutiny. However, she let it pass.

"You're quite right. I am here to talk about what happened to Fern. My apologies for getting sidetracked."

I saw the tension ease from Blake's body. He might not have been so quick to relax had he known Dusty better. Sooner or later she'd pry out of him what she wanted to know. For the moment though, she moved on to Blake's second wife.

"Let me start by offering you my condolences."

Blake took one last look at the navigation panels and returned to the lounge area. "Thank you. I appreciate your saying that. I'm through being treated like a suspect without any thought I might be grieving. I loved Tiri. I missed her a lot. I still miss her. We had something special." He slipped back into his seat. "I also loved Fern." His half smile suggested he understood that might sound like a contradiction.

"It must have been disconcerting for you to meet Inspector Lyons again, this time as the investigator of your second wife's murder."

"I admit I was uncomfortable at first with the way she did her level best to find evidence to prove I'd killed Fern. But I don't hold that against her. She was merely doing her job just as she was when she tried to save Tiri without a thought for her own safety. I'll always respect her for that."

"I understand you've already given a statement to the police, but I need you to tell me what you were doing the evening Fern died – say between 10.30 and 11.30."

"You're right. I'm through repeating myself. But if it can help in any way…" Dusty waited. "Okay. I'd had a bit too much to drink that evening. Fern and I had been out to a local restaurant earlier. Our relationship was going through a rough patch. To be honest, *I* was going through a rough patch."

"Because you were back in Broome facing your demons?"

Blake gave Dusty a look that expressed both surprise and appreciation of her astuteness.

"Something like that. You see, I was in the process of writing my memoirs, still am as a matter of fact. It seemed like the right time. It had been seventeen years since Tiri died. I felt enough time had passed for me to write about that period of my life. I was in a new relationship, a good marriage. I thought I could write about difficult times from a comfortable place."

"It didn't work out the way you expected?"

"It did at first. But when it came to writing about those last few weeks with Tiri, I got stuck; dried up. Like you, Fern felt I had demons to exorcise. It was her idea to come and live here in Broome – at least for a few years. *Face your fears and they'll go away*, she said. Unfortunately, being here seemed to make things worse."

"If you look for her, you'll lose her forever."

Blake's brow furrowed.

"Orpheus," explained Dusty. "He loved a woman of extraordinary beauty. When Eurydice died, Orpheus went into deep mourning. The only thing he wanted was to see his wife again. The gods took pity on him. They gave him permission to go to Hades and bring Eurydice back from the dead. He was warned he must not look for her to check if she was coming. If he did, she would be lost forever."

"You could be right. Maybe I'm afraid of losing Tiri forever." Blake spread his hands out on the table and drummed his fingers. His familiar broad grin signalled the end of sombre discussion. "Time for lunch."

# CHAPTER 14

AFTER A LAST check that all was well on the instrument panels, Blake took us down to the galley.

He once more adopted the role of proud host, pointing out the full-size microwave and oven, a gas stove top, a dishwasher and garbage compacter, freezer, pull-out pantry shelves. "We can latch everything that needs to be secured."

He unlatched a cabinet and opened it to reveal a well stocked fridge.

"I made these for us earlier," he said, removing a platter piled high with sandwiches and passing it to Dusty.

Reaching back into the fridge, he withdrew a tray with an assortment of savoury items such as olives and anchovies which he handed to me. The final item was a bottle of chilled wine. He placed it in a basket already stacked with cutlery and plates.

"Let's eat alfresco," he said. "There's not much of a wind at the moment; we'll be comfortable out in the open."

As we followed Blake up the stairs, Dusty's comment about being out in the middle of the ocean with a murderer came into my mind. For a brief moment I wondered about the sandwiches. Why did he make them in advance? Were they laced with something? Did our charming host plan on putting us to sleep to render us incapable of struggling so he could throw us overboard? Didn't Dusty say something about Blake Montgomery using his charm and intelligence to get away with murder? Not for the first time, I berated myself for being fanciful. Even if Blake had murdered his wife, why would he want to kill Dusty and me? Besides, he'd shown genuine concern earlier when he realised Dusty had been wandering around outside without a vest.

I slid into a chair at the table on the boat deck. Once I'd vanquished my flights of fancy, I settled into the very agreeable experience of enjoying a hearty lunch.

"Such a spacious yacht." Dusty's appreciative glance took in her surroundings. "Almost room to play golf on this deck."

Blake laughed. "I like a game of golf, but not on board the boat. Most of the golf balls would end up in the ocean. I don't think Doris or her sea nymphs would appreciate that."

Dusty's face remained impassive but under the table her foot tapped the side of my leg.

Keeping my tone casual, I asked the question Dusty was prompting me to ask. "Does Broome have a golf course?"

"Super golf course. I keep my gear there in a locker." Blake's eyes met mine. "Including my clubs, of course." I had the impression his smile, though apparently winsome, was intended to goad me. A current of fear zapped through me, causing the skin on my scalp to prickle. Did he know Dusty had searched his cabin? Was he gloating because he'd been one step ahead of her?

When Blake proceeded to tell us about some of the incredible golf courses he'd played on as a result of sailing the world's oceans, he sounded so natural and amiable my foolish apprehension vanished. The sandwiches, the excellent wine and the surreal experience of eating lunch on the luxury yacht of a Hollywood movie star now absorbed my attention.

Shortly after our meal, we were treated to one of those moments people dream of when they head out into the open sea; a close encounter with marine animals. Concerned about a change in wind conditions, Blake was back at the helm. He'd altered course to return to Broome when he spotted a pod of dolphins with his binoculars.

"Now there's a rare sight," he said, pointing ahead. "A pod of snubfin dolphins or snubbies as some Aussies call them."

He suggested Dusty and I go back out on deck to get a better view. After the stable comfort of the cockpit, the wind took me by surprise when we stepped onto the deck. I was glad we had followed

Blake's instructions to wear safety vests.

"Interesting about his golf clubs," said Dusty. We were leaning against the rail with our backs to the pilot house as we waited for the yacht to get closer to the dolphins.

When the boat drew parallel with the creatures, they seemed unperturbed about our presence. They swam beside the *Doris*, leaping in and out of the water in pairs and groups.

"Oh…my…god!" Dusty jumped up and down like an excited child.

One of the dolphins swam up to the yacht and leapt out of the water so close to us we could almost touch its melon-shaped head. After landing back in the ocean it executed a sharp turn on the surface, splashing salty water at us with its tail. Dusty and I grabbed the rail along the side of the yacht to reduce the risk of being swept overboard. Once again, I thought of how easy it would be to disappear at sea.

When the whole pod of snubbies performed a stunning synchronised leap over the water with their backs to us and swam away, we reluctantly bid farewell to them. After such an exhilarating experience, the unpleasant subject of murder seemed incongruous. Dusty had relaxed into the ocean experience. Instead of returning to the subject of his dead wives when we were back in the wheelhouse, she asked Blake about his autobiography.

"Why write your memoir yourself? Don't most celebrities use ghost writers?"

If Blake interpreted Dusty's questions as a slight on his writing ability, he didn't show it.

Switching the yacht to auto pilot, he swivelled around to face us. "Y'know, I've got the next best thing; an extremely efficient assistant with broad experience in helping people write their autobiographies. She goes over what I've written and manages to improve it quite a bit." The now familiar broad grin acknowledged his skills as a writer might not match those he displayed on screen as an actor.

"It's always good to have an objective critic." If Blake was hoping Dusty had lost her focus on Fern, he was quickly disabused. "Did you and Fern argue when you got back to the yacht the evening she was murdered?" Until that moment, Blake had seemed in his element and free of worries. Now a sober expression clouded his face. Dusty's question had jolted him back to the real world. However, he answered without trying to prevaricate.

"Not at all. We were enjoying a drink together. Fern had opened a bottle of Prosecco. I was making my way too fast through a bottle of scotch. I knew things were not right between us but I just couldn't start the conversation. Y'know what I mean?"

Dusty nodded. I did too, thinking of the conversation I had long yearned to have with Dusty.

"The more I put it off," continued Blake, "the more I drank."

"Fern didn't ask you to slow down with your drinking?"

Blake shook his head. "It wasn't as if I was going to take the boat out or drive a car."

A concerned wife might have urged her husband to be careful of excessive drinking for health reasons. I wondered if Fern had encouraged Blake to drink knowing he would eventually fall into a deep sleep, leaving the way clear for her to rendezvous with her lover.

"Did you know Fern was planning on going out to meet someone that night?"

Blake turned to gaze through one of the side windows, his jaw clenched. After a moment, while still staring out at the ocean, he shook his head.

"Did you know your wife was having an affair?"

Blake swivelled his chair around to the front, turning his back to us. He made a show of checking the displays before facing us again, his expression impassive.

"I'm sorry, Blake. I need to ask these questions. You didn't suspect anything at all?"

"I was going through a difficult time. I thought Fern was giving me space to sort myself out. I didn't find out she was having an affair until after her death."

"And you found out who she'd been seeing?"

Blake scowled. "The personal trainer at Tranquillity. If I was going to murder anyone it would have been him, not my wife. Fern was a wonderful lady."

When Dusty asked Blake, 'just for the record', where he was when Fern died, he sighed with weary acceptance.

"Here on *Doris*, on that sofa over there, sleeping off the effects of a bottle of scotch. I didn't move until the police arrived to tell me about Fern." Blake shifted the focus from his movements on the night of Fern's death to the progress of the investigation. "Dusty, I know you haven't been on the case for very long, but have you formed an opinion about who murdered Fern?"

Dusty offered him a cautious response. "It's too early for me to draw any conclusions. However, the police have ruled out a serial killer. They're convinced the two murders after Fern were copycat killings."

"Which leaves the question of who murdered my wife. And why." Blake's mouth was set in a determined line as if he knew the answer to that question and intended to do something about it. I couldn't help wondering whether I was seeing a sincere grieving husband or an accomplished actor.

# CHAPTER 15

BACK AT THE marina, Dusty and I sprang into our deckhand roles hanging out the slip ropes and tying them once the yacht was docked. On completion, we stood back and looked at our handiwork, giving each other the thumbs-up for having followed the skipper's instructions well enough to complete what looked like a reasonably good job. When Blake joined us on the deck, I helped him reconnect the power line. We'd just finished when he waved to someone approaching in the distance.

"That's Kayla Bassett, the lady who helps me knock my writing into shape. The Australian arm of my publisher sent her to work with me. I'm very glad they did. She's invaluable."

Striding towards the yacht was a slim brunette dressed in a conservative black jacket, pencil skirt and heels that elevated her height to around five-foot-nine. The black document folder she carried in one hand matched her shoulder bag. Her medium length thick hair bounced as she walked. Had she been aware of it, I think she would have found a way to keep it still, to bring it in line with her executive appearance.

"I'd like to have a quick word with your Personal Assistant," said Dusty, taking her leave of Blake. "We'll introduce ourselves."

I realised Dusty was seizing the opportunity to speak to Blake's PA without him being present. She reached Kayla Bassett as the other woman drew level with the docking pen next to the one the *Doris* was moored at.

Kayla's sombre countenance as Dusty put out her hand in an introductory handshake suggested this was a woman who didn't like surprises being sprung on her. Burgundy lipstick matching the colour of the narrow frames of her glasses suggested a no-nonsense attitude. I half expected her to reprimand us for disrupting her regular routine.

However, she relaxed somewhat as Dusty made the introductions, although her expression remained guarded.

"You're here to investigate the murder of Fern Parkes?"

"We are. I'd like to ask you a few questions if you don't mind."

"If it will assist you find out who the murderer is, I'll do anything I can."

Dusty began in an amiable tone. "I was reluctant to mention this to Blake, but I wondered about his other yacht; the one he and Tiri were on the night she died. What happened to the *Tooting Moon*?"

"Mr Montgomery couldn't face sailing in it after the accident. I wasn't working with him at the time but he has mentioned it. He flew back to the United States after Tiri died and left the yacht moored here but never sailed it again. He donated *Tooting Moon* to the Broome council so they could sell it and raise money to make improvements to Queen City Marina. He won't crow about it but this magnificent marina with the cafes and retail precinct is thanks to Mr Montgomery. Because of him, this area is now prime real estate. That should give you some idea of what sort of person he is." Kayla fixed Dusty with an earnest stare. "He's not a murderer. It's terrible to think he has to endure innuendo and suspicion all over again."

"Terrible for Fern too; she lost her life."

If Blake's PA picked up the criticism in Dusty's statement, she didn't let it show. "Of course. No one deserves to have their life cut short. But my main concern is with the living."

Clearly, Kayla didn't feel warm affection for Fern. Dusty was quick to take advantage.

"What sort of person was Fern?"

"I had very little to do with her." Sensing Kayla could reveal insights into Fern's character, Dusty persisted.

"Was she a devoted wife?"

Kayla didn't respond. However, the tightening of her lips was answer enough.

"I know she was having an affair." Dusty lowered her voice as a group of inquisitive tourists strolled past. "Aside from that, or before that, was she committed to her marriage? I mean, as far as you knew, was she often unfaithful to her husband?"

Behind the lenses of her glasses, Kayla blinked. "I don't see how prying into their personal lives can help you find out who killed the poor woman. I really must go. Mr Montgomery and I have a lot of work to do today." To emphasise the point, she raised the document folder and made to pass us. Dusty's next words caused her to hesitate.

"I have good reasons for asking these intrusive questions." Kayla gave her a sceptical look. "I'm trying to find out whether someone else connected with Fern might have had reason to kill her, someone other than her husband." Dusty now had the woman's full attention. "At this stage, it looks very much like Blake Montgomery killed his wife."

This elicited an immediate sharp response. "That's where you're wrong, Miss Kent." Kayla's jaw jutted forward. "Mr Montgomery is not a killer. I can prove it."

Dusty raised her eyebrows. "What do you mean?"

"He was on the *Doris* at the time his wife was murdered." A blush tinged the PA's cheeks.

Dusty put her head to one side, studying Kayla's face. "I'm aware he told the police that. The problem is, there's no-one to corroborate it."

"There certainly is. I can corroborate his story, as you put it." Kayla hugged the document bag against her chest. "I came back to the yacht that evening. For some papers. Mr Montgomery and I had been working on his manuscript during the day. I was at home revising it when I realised I needed some of his handwritten notes. I wanted to transfer them to my computer before we began work the next day. He was passed out on the couch when I arrived." The memory of a sleeping Blake Montgomery caused an unexpectedly pretty smile to soften Kayla's expression.

"What time was this?"

"I know exactly what time it was because I checked before boarding the yacht. I was worried it might be too late to call on him. When I saw a couple of lights on, I thought it would be all right to go on board, excuse myself and quickly retrieve the papers."

"And the time was…?"

"Eleven o'clock."

"Why didn't you wait until morning?"

Kayla maintained eye contact with Dusty but the pink in her cheeks deepened. "It would have been too late. I needed to have the manuscript ready before we started working on it the next day."

Her statement fitted with my perception of her. Kayla would consider it a matter of personal pride to be up to date and prepared. However, I wondered at her apparent embarrassment. Was she lying?

"How long did you stay on the yacht?"

"About fifteen or twenty minutes. It took me a while to find the notes I wanted." Kayla swallowed and took a breath before continuing. "After I found them, I stood out on the deck for a few minutes to enjoy the balmy evening."

"Blake didn't wake up while you were there?"

"No. He was snoring the whole time." Her lips set in a determined line. "If you want me to swear to it, I will."

"Why didn't you tell the police you could alibi Blake?"

"I didn't see any need to. I didn't believe for one minute they'd seriously consider him a suspect. If the police had laid charges, naturally I would have come forward." Kayla straightened. "I'd best get on."

"More of a German shepherd than a basset hound, don't you think?" Dusty watched Kayla striding toward the *Doris*. "Loyal protector and erect posture rather than soft and floppy."

I had no idea why Dusty was comparing Blake's Personal Assistant to dogs. My bewilderment must have shown on my face.

"Her name," prompted Dusty. "Blake said her name was Bassett."

"Right. Bassett. Got it! Bassett hound."

"On the other hand she is soft in one way." Dusty turned. We began to stroll along the boardwalk toward the retail precinct watching the sea birds flying between the masts of the moored yachts and calling to each other. "She's soft on Blake."

"How'd you work that out?"

Dusty responded with a quizzical look. "Haven't I taught you anything, Mr Maze Master?" This was accompanied by a teasing grin.

"Evidently not. What did I miss?"

"The most important clue was the change in her tone of voice. Didn't you notice the tender inflection whenever she spoke about 'Mr Montgomery'? Why do you think she spent so much time on the yacht the night she went to pick up the papers?" Dusty didn't wait for an answer. "Because she was, for the briefest of time, fantasising she was Mrs Montgomery enjoying a balmy evening on their yacht. And why didn't she speak up to the police? Because she was embarrassed. I'm guessing she stayed on the yacht for much longer than twenty minutes that night. I wouldn't mind betting she sat and solicitously watched her sleeping 'husband'." Dusty raised her fingers to bracket the last word. "The efficient PA wasn't entirely truthful. She's holding something back, no doubt to protect Blake Montgomery."

"Right. So she lied about going to the yacht to pick up some papers?"

"She seems to be telling the truth about that." Dusty sighed and added, "Unfortunately."

The last thing Dusty expected was for Blake to have an alibi. Although it was not like her to become fixated on a suspect, she hadn't questioned Blake's guilt. Now she had to re-evaluate her opinion of him and re-assess the case.

A thoughtful expression crossed her face as we walked past the shops through to the car park. "To tell you the truth, for a while out there on the ocean, I began to think Blake might be the devoted husband he claims to have been." I had noticed how Dusty had seemed to warm to our skipper.

"Now Kayla's alibi confirms that?"

"Not necessarily. When I was tempted to succumb to his charm, I reminded myself he's an experienced actor."

"Right. Did you switch on the Dusty Kent Lie Detector?"

Dusty grinned. "I did. Blake Montgomery might have an alibi for the time of Fern's death but he's not telling the whole truth about the night Tiri died. That much I'm sure of."

# CHAPTER 16

"WHAT MADE YOU think I was a man?"

Jack was referring to the day I'd seen the 'lurking man' at Pearl's Shell.

It was now mid morning on Sunday, two days after our adventure on Blake Montgomery's luxury yacht. The three of us were sitting in the covered outdoor area of the beach house under cooling fans with a jug of iced water to sustain us as we assessed our progress in the case.

Having adjusted to the leisurely pace of 'Broome time' we had each started the morning without haste. Mine began with a stroll along the beach where the early sun cast long shadows across the sand and the surf licked the shore. Shortly after I returned, Dusty had skipped down the stairs in her bikini with a towel over her shoulders to take a dip in the pool. Jack had emerged from her room, yawning and rubbing her eyes, in time to join us for a late breakfast in the town.

I contemplated Jack's question before answering. "I suppose because you were dressed like a man."

Jack ran a hand through her spiked white hair. "T-shirt and shorts? Coulda been a woman. Something else?"

Dusty, her eyes on me in anticipation of my response, poured us each a glass of water.

"Right." I cast my mind back to the day at Pearl's Shell when I'd mistaken Jack for a man. What was it that caused me to assume her gender was male? "The baseball cap and the sunglasses made me think of a guy. Then I saw your tattooed calves. All of these things suggested a man. And you were scratching your groin area."

Jack clapped her hands. "Nice touch, don't you think? If you'll pardon the pun. Anything else?"

An image flashed into my mind when Jack had raised her arms to clap. "You were wearing a man's watch. I don't remember noticing it at the time but I must have at some level."

"Aha. The chunky watch sends a subtle message to the subconscious."

Dusty smiled at me over her coffee cup. "You see how clever she is."

"Did you have Spratt with you?" I wondered what she did with her pet when she was on the job.

"Nup. He was still here fast asleep in his cosy pouch." Jack had fashioned a sleeping pouch for her tiny pet from a knitted tea cosy. "He prefers my bra but I can't always let him sleep there." Jack grinned and stroked her left breast where Spratt was in deep slumber.

Dusty patted the case files on the table in front of her. "Okay, team. Let's see where we're at."

Jack put her hand up. "Wanna hear my report on the famous Hollywood star?"

She reached into a deep pocket of her hippie dress and drew out a bedraggled pad of paper, the loose leaves struggling to stay contained. We had seen little of Jack over the past few days while she'd been out 'gathering intelligence' during the day and 'tracking suspects' at night. Her system of recording the information she had gleaned didn't look particularly organised.

Dusty glanced at Jack's 'filing system', a tolerant smile on her lips. "Let's do a recap first."

An expression of mock disappointment passed over Jack's face as she made a show of being disgruntled. She placed her notes back on the table and attempted to pat them into a neat stack but failed, giving up with a shrug.

"First, let's look at what we know about Fern's murder. She was killed on Thursday January twelfth while walking from the Montgomery private yacht to another yacht at the other end of Queen City Marina where her lover Wasim Smith was waiting. Fern was murdered sometime between 10.45pm when she texted her lover to tell him she was on the way and 11.15pm when her body was discovered by a passer-by. She had been struck over the head from behind then strangled. Police found no evidence to link Blake Montgomery to his wife's murder." Dusty cast a doleful glance at Jack. "Unfortunately, our prime suspect has an alibi for the time of the murder." She held up a hand to silence Jack's protest. "I'm not giving up on Blake Montgomery just yet. He claims he wasn't aware of Fern's affair, but I'm not convinced he's telling the truth."

Jack snorted so loudly I thought Spratt would wake up. A quick glance at the left side of Jack's chest confirmed he hadn't stirred.

"If Blake Montgomery didn't know what his wife was up to, he must have been the only person in Broome who didn't," said Jack. "Wasim Smith and Fern were discreet but in a small place like this it's hard to keep secrets."

Dusty acknowledged Jack's point with a nod and continued. "If Blake deliberately killed Tiri seventeen years ago because he believed she was unfaithful then passed it off as an accident, he could have done the same thing to his second wife. It's possible he and Fern had a fight that night because he confronted her about her affair. Only this time, instead of passing it off as an accident, he decided to pass it off as murder; murder by a random attacker."

Knowing Jack and Dusty had virtually made up their minds about Blake, I decided it was up to me to point out the flaws in their theory.

"Creeping up behind her to knock her over the head suggests stealth. Right? Doesn't sound like the behaviour of a man in the heat of passionate anger."

Dusty's rebuttal was swift. "Maybe she fell on the yacht and knocked her head. He panicked. He may have even thought she was dead. So he strangled her to make it look like murder and put her body in the alleyway."

"Why didn't he throw her overboard and let the police assume it was an accident which happened while he was sleeping off his drinking binge? If she was unconscious from the bump on the head, she'd drown once she was in the water."

Dusty shook her head. "Too much like Tiri Welsh's drowning. The police might not believe him a second time. Blake Montgomery would have been clever enough not to murder his second wife the same way as his first. He might have pretended to be asleep then waited for her to leave and followed her. Domestic violence murders are not necessarily committed as a result of spontaneous rage. In fact, most of them involve planning."

I wasn't ready to give up. "If he killed her on the yacht, getting her body off the boat and carrying her to the alleyway would be risky. Bound to be people around at that time, coming and going to the other yachts or returning to their cars from Diamond Box Cocktail Bar. Besides, didn't the forensic evidence indicate Fern was murdered where she was found?"

Dusty flicked through the police file. When she located the page she wanted, she scanned it.

"It says she was, *in all likelihood*, murdered in the alleyway. But that's not conclusive."

I wondered why Dusty was finding it so difficult to accept the possibility Blake Montgomery might be innocent of murdering his second wife. As usual, I failed to keep my thoughts from appearing on my face. Dusty responded as if I'd spoken them.

"All right, maybe I'm clutching at straws." She cast a hopeful glance at Jack. "What did you find out about him?"

Jack patted her pile of paper with a sad shake of the head. "Where he's concerned, I haven't dug up any dirt. He leads a quiet life on his boat. Apart from the yacht and his obviously expensive clothes, you wouldn't know he was a famous film star. He rides a bike around town to the bank and places like that but has most of his supplies delivered. Sometimes meets with a few of the local business people for dinner. Sometimes has visitors from overseas staying with him on the yacht. After Fern's funeral in America, his fifteen-year-old daughter Cindy came back from the UK where she attends school, and stayed for a couple of weeks on the *Doris* with her father. He's well-liked by the locals. Spends most of his time working on his biography with his assistant. Pretty boring life for a Hollywood star. In fact he's so ordinary, it makes me wonder what he's hiding."

"What about his assistant; his loyal PA?"

Jack glanced at her notes. "Her name's Kayla Bassett."

"Yes. Sean and I met her. Anything going on between her and Blake?"

"Doesn't look like it," said Jack. "She's there every week day and occasionally works late on the yacht with him. They sometimes share a drink out on the deck but she never stays the night."

Dusty looked thoughtful. "There's something in the back of my mind about Kayla Bassett that's niggling at me. I can't quite put my finger on what it is." She ran both hands through her hair, lifting it up with her fingers and letting the spirals of curls fall down again. "Never mind, it'll come to me eventually." She cast a glance in my direction. "What have you found out about Broome's resident movie star, Mr Maze Master?"

I wasn't able to offer anything further on Blake Montgomery. I'd sent out a couple of emails to contacts in the United States but they hadn't come up with anything worthwhile at this stage.

Dusty threw her arms in the air. "Let's leave Blake for the moment. Time to take a closer look at his 'understudy'."

# CHAPTER 17

"SOMETHING ON YOUR mind?"

It was the following day. I was behind the wheel of Dusty's car, driving to Fern's wellness centre to interview Wasim Smith. In the passenger seat, Dusty had been uncharacteristically quiet.

She responded to my question with an appraising look. "You know me so well, Sean."

Her comment sent a frisson of pleasure through my body. It was a tantalising hint that she felt close to me. However, I didn't really know her well. Dusty was an enigma to me and no doubt always would be.

She turned to observe the passing scenery through the passenger side window. "I was giving myself a good telling off in my mind for being a nincompoop. Since Day One I've been convinced Blake Montgomery was a murderer and all I had to do was prove it. I should have kept an open mind from the start."

"You usually do."

"Exactly why I'm so annoyed with myself."

"No worries, mate." I did my best imitation of a broad Australian accent which caused a slow smile to warm her face. I continued. "We've only just started the investigation so no harm done. Right?"

I slowed the car to turn into an open entrance flanked by thick sandstone gateposts. The double wrought iron gates that had been opened and secured on either side both bore the name Tranquillity in elegant script.

"True. But I have to start doing my job properly. I need to focus on finding out who murdered Fern Parkes. Her lover is as good a place to start as any. Maybe she went to meet him that night to break off the affair and he ended up strangling her as Inspector Lyons suggested."

As we progressed along the broad driveway, past ancient trees on both sides, Dusty glanced around in awe of the lush bush setting. "Look at this place! It looks too lush for an arid area like Broome." We wound down the car windows to breathe in the outside air which was fresh and natural with a faint tinge of eucalyptus. The driveway ended in a circular turn. I parked the car to one side, allowing room for other cars to get past if necessary.

Birds called to each other in the distance as we strolled along a cobblestone path to a simple wooden building with a homestead style verandah. The approach to the front entrance was from the side where white stone steps led to a wide patio. Recliners waited for occupants. A peacock, his tail trailing behind him, strutted with nonchalant disdain along the edge of a reflection pool bordering the front of the patio. He passed us without a second glance as we approached the glass front doors.

Shiny wooden floors, white paintwork and opulent chandelier light fittings greeted us inside. Stairs led up to rooms with glass walls where we could see a yoga class in progress in one room and a tai chi class in another.

We had called ahead to let Fern's friend Shama Vellu know we were coming. She was the manager of Tranquillity. When she swept toward us now, I realised I had seen her before.

Her warm smile greeted us. "Welcome to Tranquillity."

"Didn't we see you at Pearl's Shell the other day?" said Dusty.

"You did. I'm a volunteer there."

She was the attractive dark-skinned woman we had seen exchanging greetings with Rhona by the coffee machine.

With a sweeping hand gesture, Shama invited us to tour Tranquillity.

"It looks impressive. But business first, I think." Dusty came straight to the point. "I understand Blake Montgomery might have had good reason to be jealous in his marriage."

Shama lowered her head. "You mean because Fern was having an affair?"

"Correct. I believe her lover works here. I'd like to see him, if I may."

Shama pointed to a room on the upper level fitted out with various exercise machines. "Wasim is finishing up with a client." A muscular man in his late twenties wearing a sleeveless red T-shirt and black shorts was holding a slim, fair-haired woman by the ankles while she finished a stomach press. When he released her, she sprang to her feet.

"You can talk to him up there if you like. I've already told him about you and why you're here in Broome."

We took the stairs and arrived at the room as the fair-haired woman was leaving, a gym bag over her shoulder. Wasim, who was on his knees adjusting the exercise mat, stood up as Dusty and I entered. He was dark skinned with a powerfully built frame and black hair shaved close except for a spiky clump running along the top of his scalp. He looked no more than twenty five but was probably older. Nevertheless, he must have been quite a bit younger than forty-one-year-old Fern. Despite the fact that he stood several inches shorter than I, he had an intimidating presence. Until his boyish smile softened that image.

After we'd introduced ourselves, Dusty explained she was in Broome to investigate Fern's murder.

"Shama told me. Happy to help if I can." Wasim bent over to roll up the exercise mat. He placed it on a shelf alongside several others.

"How long have you been in Australia?" Dusty was either genuinely interested or was making conversation to relax him.

"Accent gives me away, eh?" His boyish smile lit up his face again. "Been here five or six years I reckon."

I hadn't noticed anything different about his accent but now, having been alerted, I recognised the vowel sounds of a New Zealander. I should have picked it up sooner. My fiancé Ingrid was born 'across the ditch', as they say here in Australia. Although she's lived here since she was a child, her Kiwi accent is still discernible.

"Hope you catch Fern's killer," continued Wasim. "The police have done bugger all."

Ingrid had told me New Zealanders call a spade a spade. So do Australians, generally, but Dusty respected the hard work of police officers and leapt to their defence. "The task force working on Fern's case did a great deal; they just haven't been able to find enough evidence to arrest anyone."

"Her husband, you mean?"

"Why do you say that?"

Wasim shrugged. He moved away to straighten a set of brightly coloured barbells.

"I know you and Fern were having an affair," said Dusty.

Wasim turned to face us. "Not an affair exactly." Noticing Dusty's puzzled frown, he elaborated. "I mean, it wasn't a love affair or anything."

"What was it then?"

Wasim folded his muscular arms across his chest. "Just…you know. Just sex, really."

"So you weren't in love with her?"

He ran a hand through the spiked strip of hair on the top of his head. "Has this got anything to do with catching the person who killed her?"

Dusty fixed him with a searching look. Wasim averted his eyes. I wondered why he found the subject of love between him and Fern uncomfortable. Had she been in love with him and wanted more than 'just sex'? Did that lead to problems he didn't want Dusty to find out about?

"You said you were happy to help."

"Yeah. But this…this is personal stuff. What's it got to do with her death?"

"The thing is, Blake Montgomery has an alibi for the time Fern was killed. So I'm looking for another suspect."

It took a moment for the innuendo to hit home. "Me?" His eyes widened, making him look like an innocent young boy. "Me?"

"Most women are killed by men, usually men they know. You were her lover. Where were you the night Fern was killed?"

Dusty already knew the answer to this question from the police reports, but she liked to get first-hand responses.

"I was at the marina waiting for Fern."

"You own a yacht?"

"I wish!" Wasim laughed. "It's a friend's boat. He sometimes has to fly to Perth for work. When he's not in town he lets me use his yacht. It's a great place for…" he shrugged, "you know."

"Where was this yacht moored?"

"At the end of the pier where the two boardwalks meet."

"So not far from where the *Doris* was moored?"

Wasim's smile acknowledged the irony of carrying on an affair with a woman whose husband was in such close proximity.

"Fern liked to meet me there." He looked down at the floor, tracing the line of a floorboard with the toe of his shoe. "She got a kick out of it."

"Because of the risk of being found out?"

Wasim nodded. "I'd have been happier further away but…" he paused, looking bashful as he reached up to rub the back of his neck. "But I have to admit, it did raise the level of excitement."

I sensed excitement was something Wasim revelled in. It wasn't difficult to imagine him bungee jumping, sky diving or paragliding.

"Blake never suspected?"

"Reckon I'd have known about it if he had. He has a bit of a temper on him according to Fern. Besides, most of the time we…" he glanced around, "we got together here during the day. Her husband rarely came here. We only met at the marina when I had the use of my friend's yacht. Fern used to wait until hubby was out of it. Then she'd text me to tell me she was on her way."

"She didn't go directly to the yacht where you were, did she?"

"Nope. She went through the alley to the other end of the cafe precinct to make it look like she was going to the car park behind the cafes. Then she'd walk along the precinct and approach my friend's yacht from that direction. She sort of dressed down to reduce the risk of being recognised. It was a bit of a game."

"I see. I suppose that added to the excitement."

"Fern…" Wasim's tone was conspiratorial but he decided not to continue.

Dusty, sensing a potential revelation, prompted him. "Yes? What were you going to say?"

He kept his eyes averted. "I miss her. That's all."

Dusty retreated but I knew she'd try to tease out whatever it was he'd been about to reveal. Anything a witness was trying to hide was buried treasure to Dusty.

"So Fern texted you that night. Told you she was on her way and headed off through the alley." The police had recovered the text message prudently deleted by Fern. "Why do you think she used the alley instead of the new walkway?"

Wasim shrugged. "Maybe to avoid meeting anyone and being recognised."

"Do you know if she always went that way?"

"Dunno. I didn't go to meet her. We kept it low key. I usually stayed on the yacht until she arrived." He closed his eyes and pinched the bridge of his nose. Was he trying to hold back tears?

Dusty threw in a direct question designed to catch him off balance. "Did you strangle Fern?"

"Strangle?" Wasim's confusion whirled around in his eyes before merging with alarm. Was he afraid Dusty had evidence to prove his guilt? Realising she'd struck a nerve, Dusty pressed her advantage.

"Were you waiting for Fern in the alley? Did you sneak up behind her and kill her?"

Wasim's panic was replaced by anger. Whether it was sincere rage or a mask to hide his fear, I could not tell. "What the... Why on earth would I do that? You must be outa your mind." A red flush deepened his dark complexion.

"Maybe Fern wasn't on her way to meet you at all. Did she have a new man? Perhaps she was going to the car park to drive to her new lover's place."

Wasim shook his head.

"You were in love with her and angry at being rejected, passed over for another. You decided if you couldn't have her, no-one could."

Wasim walked over to the glass wall. He looked down on the reception area below with his back to us, tension and defiance in his rigid posture. Finally, he turned around.

"We weren't in love."

Dusty put her head to one side, looking at him quizzically. This wasn't what she had expected him to say.

"Fern…" Wasim's voice had the same conspiratorial tone as before. Dusty waited, anticipating that this time he would follow through with whatever it was he'd been going to reveal earlier.

"Fern had urges which needed to be gratified." He paused as though expecting an objection. When Dusty gave no sign of disapproval, he continued. "It might seem disrespectful to speak of her that way; I don't mean any disrespect whatsoever. The truth is, Fern had a high sex drive. Her husband wasn't…wasn't coming to the party, so to speak. I wasn't emotionally involved. I mean, I liked her and I really enjoyed what we had. That's all there was to it. If she had decided to be with someone else, I'd have been disappointed. But it wouldn't have broken my heart."

"Still, you can see how it looks. Apart from anything else, you don't have an alibi for the time Fern was murdered."

"I do have an alibi. I was talking to someone while I was waiting for Fern. I told the police that. When she didn't turn up at the yacht after she texted, I went outside and looked along the boardwalk to see if she was coming. I got talking to a guy who was on his way to one of the other yachts, I think. We passed the time together until around midnight."

"The problem is the police were never able to track this guy you say you were talking to."

"They didn't try hard enough." Wasim's face set in a defiant expression.

# CHAPTER 18

WE WERE FOLLOWING Wasim down the stairs a few minutes later when Dusty caught my attention with a light touch of my arm and a nod toward the front door. Blake Montgomery had just walked in. His relaxed demeanour changed immediately he caught sight of Wasim. Rage blazed in his dark eyes.

Fists clenched, he marched in a determined line right up to Wasim, who had just reached the bottom of the stairs. A vein in Blake's neck throbbed.

"You!" Blake jabbed a finger at the personal trainer. "You killed her, didn't you?"

Having witnessed quite a few fights during my stint as a barman when I first arrived in Australia, I knew this situation could escalate at the slightest provocation. I willed Wasim to stay silent. Thankfully, he did. He moved back a step but that was as far as he could go without going back up the stairs. From my brief meeting with Wasim I judged he would not choose to retreat.

"You did! I can see it in your eyes. You snivelling little pipsqueak."

That was too much for Wasim. He was no pipsqueak. He was shorter than Blake but he had the muscle power to overcome the older man with ease. With body tensed and fists clenched, he widened the gap between his feet and placed one foot slightly forward.

Without hesitation, I placed myself between the two men, facing Blake. In my haste, I didn't notice Wasim had already started to bring his fist up to strike Blake. By moving in front of him I had placed myself in his line of fire. Fortunately, as I learned later, Dusty with her quick reflexes and karate training, blocked Wasim's swinging arm before the fist at the end of it could slam into my body. I remained blissfully unaware of what had transpired behind me and focused on calming Blake.

"Is this the right way to honour Fern's memory?" I spoke in a quiet tone, knowing another raised voice would only exacerbate the heightened state of both men.

At that moment, Shama appeared. "Please, Blake. Walk away."

Blake rounded on her. "Why is this…this individual still working here?" He jerked his head at Wasim.

Shama took Blake's arm. "Let's talk about this in my office." After flinging one last furious glare at Wasim, Blake allowed Shama to lead him aside. The tension began to ease from Wasim's body. He relaxed his stance.

After giving him several more seconds to regain his composure, Dusty addressed him. "Blake asked you if you'd killed his wife. Did you?"

Wasim folded his powerful arms across his chest. "Like I said, Fern and I had a good thing going. Why would I want to murder her?"

"Because you were in love with her." Glistening beads of perspiration appeared on Wasim's forehead. Dusty glanced at me, triumph gleaming in her eyes. "But she wouldn't leave her husband. In fact, she'd decided to break it off with you. You couldn't handle that."

Wasim's defiance dissipated. He threw his arms in the air. "All right. I was in love with her."

This took me by surprise. Wasim had sounded so plausible when he spoke about his relationship with Fern as being 'just sex' but Dusty must have ascertained he was lying.

"That's one reason," continued Wasim in a soft voice, "one very good reason why I wouldn't hurt her."

"I disagree," said Dusty. "Love is one of the main reasons people commit murder."

Wasim shot a glance in the direction of Shama's office. "You're looking in the wrong place." He made to leave. "I'm late for a meeting."

Dusty eyed his retreating back. "He's afraid of something. I can feel it."

"Afraid you'll find evidence to prove his guilt?"

"That's what I'm wondering."

Wasim's departure was timely. Blake and Shama emerged from the office as he disappeared from view around the corner of the reception area. Blake approached us and apologised for his earlier behaviour.

"No worries," said Dusty.

"He's the one the police should be investigating." Blake jerked his head at the spot where Wasim had been standing during their confrontation. "The police were too easy on him. They were so convinced I had to be the killer. It has to be the husband, right?" He gave Dusty an accusing glance. "You came straight to me too, didn't you?"

"I would have been negligent if I hadn't. By the way, was your personal assistant in the habit of visiting you on the yacht after hours?"

Blake's eyes narrowed. "What are you suggesting?"

Dusty hastened to reassure him. "I wasn't thinking of anything untoward. I only wondered if she had to return to the yacht at night for discussions or to pick up something."

"Kayla?" Blake seemed mystified. It was as though the comings and goings of his PA were so peripheral to his world he didn't notice what she was doing. Now he had to stop to think. Finally, he had an answer.

"She has come back to the boat once or twice on some errand or other. She might have left something behind after our work during the day or she might have needed to check my handwritten notes."

"Did she return to the yacht the night Fern died? I mean, after Fern left."

"You're asking the wrong person. A crowd of boozers could have come on board, raided my bar and had a party. I wouldn't have noticed – the state I was in." He extended his hands palms up with a self-effacing grin on his face. "I'm sure Kayla will be happy to tell you anything you want to know. She's incredibly organised. Y'know, she helped three Australian Prime Ministers write their autobiographies. Her experience shows. If she was on board the yacht that night, it will be documented in her notes."

After Blake left, Shama led us out to a side patio where we sat in well cushioned outdoor chairs facing the forest. Shama lifted a jug on the glass-topped oval coffee table and poured us each a long tumbler of iced water flavoured with slices of lime.

"I didn't know Blake was coming in today." She leaned over to hand us our drinks. "He wanted to pick up some of Fern's things. Poor Wasim will be worried about his job now. I'll have to reassure him. The truth is, Blake has no say over the staff arrangements or anything else to do with Tranquillity. Fern and I were equal partners in the business. Now, ownership of her share in the company has transferred to her daughter Cindy on the condition I have first option to buy her out." Shama looked across at me. "Thank you for intervening between Blake and Wasim. Apart from possibly hurting each other, physical violence is not what we want to have happening here at Tranquillity."

"I can understand that. There's a genuine ambience of peace here." Dusty paused to admire the greenery around us. "Shama, what was Fern like?"

"Beautiful looking, kind and generous. She held yoga classes and meditation sessions here at Tranquillity. Fern was exactly what you'd expect from a yoga teacher – calm and thoughtful. I never saw her ruffled."

Shama also gave the impression of not being easily flustered. Soft voice, gentle manner. I thought she might be a yoga teacher as well but when I asked, she shook her head.

"I hold silat classes." She chuckled at the bemused expressions on our faces. "Don't worry. A lot of people have never heard of it. Like many residents of Broome I'm a multi-ethnic Australian. I have Aboriginal, Filipino and Malay ancestry. The silat comes from the Malay side of my family. It's a martial art. In its purest form it can be deadly. What I teach is more of a dance. Some of the traditional silat moves are woven together in a dance routine. It's great for physical fitness."

"You and Fern obviously had similar interests. Did you see her outside work?"

"Not much. But we developed a strong bond in the work place. We often enjoyed a chat over coffee here."

"Rhona suggested you might be able to fill us in on Fern's relationship with Blake. Do you know if Blake was ever violent toward her?"

"She told me he had jealous rages that frightened her. He would yell and throw things around; champagne bottles, wine glasses, whatever was to hand. Fern denied he'd abused her physically. But I know from my work at Pearl's Shell that women often feel ashamed to admit to being abused."

"Ashamed?" I was puzzled. Why would a woman feel ashamed because some gutless bully used his physical prowess to hurt her?

Shama inclined her head to show she understood why I'd asked the question. "It sounds odd. Why should women feel ashamed in such a situation? But they do. They think people will judge them for allowing themselves to be beaten up."

Dusty looked thoughtful. "Shama, when you contacted me you said you were concerned Fern might have been killed by her husband." Shama nodded as Dusty continued. "What made you think Blake might be responsible for her murder?"

"His jealousy and because of what happened to Tiri." I wondered if Rhona had influenced Shama's prejudice against Blake, just as she had, intentionally or otherwise, prejudiced Dusty's perception of him. "I think it's possible he acted in a moment of madness, when he was incensed by jealousy. You saw today how he can flare up."

"So you think Blake found out Fern had been having an affair, erupted in a mighty rage and hit her over the head with the first thing that came to hand?" The possibility of a sock cosh being used suggested a level of premeditation rather than grabbing something on impulse, but Dusty did not mention this.

"In a state of fury, he could have lashed out at her violently."

"Do you know if Blake did find out about Fern's affair?"

The wiry tendrils of black hair framing Shama's face bounced as she shook her head. "Fern didn't say he had. That doesn't mean he didn't find out."

"Fern must have known she was taking an awful risk, starting a relationship with Wasim. Why do you think she did it?"

"She wasn't in love with Wasim. Blake lost interest in the physical side of their marriage after they came to Broome. Not completely, but enough for Fern to feel unwanted. I guess she had to prove to herself she was still attractive."

"I see. Blake mentioned their relationship was going through a rough patch."

"That's right. Fern blamed herself because coming here was her idea."

"Did Fern explain why she thought it was a good idea to come to Broome?"

"Blake was writing his memoir and he got stuck – he couldn't get past the time of Tiri's death. Fern thought coming back to where Tiri died might help him to get it out of his system."

"But things didn't turn out that way?"

Shama shook her head. "According to Fern, it made things a whole lot worse."

# CHAPTER 19

As I steered the car through the open wrought iron gates and pulled out onto the road, Dusty looked across at me. "Did you notice Wasim's reaction when I asked him if he'd strangled Fern?"

"I did. You struck fear into him." I grinned at her.

Dusty smiled, leaned back and closed her eyes. We had the road to ourselves for several kilometres. I took the opportunity to put my foot down and let the old FJ Holden show me what she could do. We passed the rest of the journey into town in companionable silence.

"Love, lust, lucre and loathing," said Dusty.

She had just finished telling Jack about our visit to Tranquillity over a late lunch at a cafe in Cable Beach. With all traces of the tattooed man gone, Jack was now herself – the eccentric hippie woman dressed in a flowing, multicoloured tie-dyed dress with her short, white hair jelled into sharp peaks. She had demolished a meal of chicken parmigiana and hot chips and now fixed an accusing stare on her plate as though it had no right to be empty. I had eaten most of my chips while they were still piping hot but had saved a few as a last tasty morsel to enjoy after my bacon and egg burger. I moved my plate further away from Jack, lifting one of the chips to my mouth as I did so.

"Lucre? What the hell is that?" Jack rarely bothered to censure her thoughts before speaking.

Dusty, who seemed to value this aspect of her friend, laughed. "Lucre is a fancy word for money. I'm quoting the great P.D. James. In one of her books a detective says those are the four motives for murder; the four Ls. He also said the most dangerous emotion is love. Wasim was in love with Fern. That gives him a motive. Especially if she broke off with him."

I sensed some hesitation in her voice. "But?"

Dusty threw her hands in the air. "I can't see him killing all three women. I wonder if we're looking for a serial killer; someone who secretly despises women and wants control over them, ultimate control by killing them."

She paused as the waitress approached. We had opted for an outdoor table well shaded by trees to mitigate the heat. Despite this, perspiration trickled down my spine. The waitress placed the second round of iced drinks Jack and I had ordered on the table. Dusty, who didn't seem to mind the heat, had chosen a pot of tea. She glanced at the notes Inspector Lyons had given her and continued.

"Some similarities suggest the same person killed all three women. No fingerprints or foreign DNA was found on any of the victims. Each victim was ambushed from behind and stunned to prevent a struggle when he strangled her. There was no sexual interference with any of the women and in each case, no attempt was made to hide or dispose of the body."

"Would a serial killer stop at three victims?" I asked. "I remember a few cases of serial killers in the UK. They seem to keep going until they're stopped."

"You're right," said Dusty. "It is odd that he stopped. But it's not beyond the realms of possibility for reasons outside his control to prevent him from continuing. Maybe he had to leave the area because of work or became incapacitated because of an accident or serious illness."

Several children, their dark skin accentuating the whiteness of their teeth as they grinned at us, ran past our table to the mini golf course. I marvelled at the way they could exert such high levels of energy despite the heat.

"Good point," I said, waving to the laughing children who were using the mini golf equipment for a game of hide and seek.

"At the end of the day, I suppose serial killers have the same restrictions of work, money or health as the rest of us." Jack was watching the children as she spoke, a wistful smile on her face. "What about the flower?" She pointed to the frangipani trees growing along the fence behind where the children were playing. "Does it give us a clue to his personality?"

"I've been thinking about that." Dusty topped up her half empty cup with more tea from the silver pot. "Why a frangipani? If it'd been a red rose it could suggest romance – a very sick concept of romance. Do frangipanis have some special meaning?"

"I'm on it." I did a quick internet search on my phone. "Right. Here we go. Frangipani, genus *plumeria*. Used as a wedding flower in parts of India, symbolises lasting bond between the couple. Swahili poets also see the frangipani as a symbol of love. Buddhist followers perceive it as a sign of immortality."

"Serious? Love? Immortality? Looks like he chose the frangipani on purpose, assuming he knew about its symbolism."

"Maybe he works in a nursery," I suggested. "That'd give him knowledge of flowers."

"Or he could have searched the internet to find a flower that served his needs. Heaps of frangipani trees grow in this area which makes it a convenient choice and untraceable as opposed to buying flowers from a florist. All he has to do is pick a flower from a tree."

"Right. Does the frangipani suggest he loves these women? Or does he believe he's giving them immortality?"

"Could be both," said Jack. "He's giving them immortality because he loves them."

"Yep! That's exactly the way that sort of twisted mind might work," said Dusty. "His choice of flower could give us a clue to who he is. A frangipani is a lovely flower so maybe he has an eye for beauty. Maybe he's connected to art in some way, or fashion or some other sort of creative endeavour."

"What about the fact he makes no attempt to hide the bodies?" I said. "Is that a clue to the sort of individual he is?"

"An interesting thought." Dusty paused to allow excited squeals from the children to subside. "It's almost as though he wants the victims to be found. He's proud of what he's achieved and wants the publicity that comes with the finding of the bodies. The fact that he didn't violate them sexually might suggest he sees women as pure, if that's the right word. He sees women as objects, not as sex objects, rather as objects of beauty, perhaps like beautiful statues, up on a pedestal."

"Why does he want to knock them off the pedestal?" I asked.

Dusty tilted her head to one side. "What if it's got something to do with his mother? Perhaps as a child he idolised his mum. Young boys often do."

I recalled how close I'd been to my own mother. I don't think I put her on a pedestal but when I was very young she was like an angel in my childish world.

Dusty interrupted my thoughts. "Do you remember the doctor, so-called doctor, in England. The one who killed hundreds of his patients?"

"Shipman?"

"Him! Apparently, as a teenager, he was at his mother's bedside when she died. Some people suggest that could be at the core of what made him do what he did. He wanted to replicate the experience."

A psychopathic killer was a possibility but I'd been wondering why there had been no rape or sexual interference.

"Could the killer have been a woman?"

"It could have been a woman." Dusty agreed, pausing in reflection for a moment. "The average female would be strong enough to strangle another woman."

"She might not be an average female," interrupted Jack. "She might be small and weak. Ambushing the victims from behind and knocking them out first is a good way of getting an advantage over a stronger person."

"Excellent point, Jack. But what would be her motive? Jealousy? Anger? Revenge? None of those are apparent in this case." In light of Dusty's analysis, I was beginning to feel embarrassed about suggesting a female killer. "And last but not least," she continued, "statistics tell us most murdered women are killed by men."

"Right. Forget my idea then."

"Not at all. We should keep an open mind. If something turns up to suggest the killer could have been a woman, we'll pursue that angle. You were right to bring it up."

Distracted by the conversation I'd forgotten about the last chips on my plate which was now empty. I looked across at Jack.

"It's a crime to let hot chips get cold," she said, licking her lips.

# CHAPTER 20

Dusty replenished her teapot with hot water and poured herself a second cup. "Remember the childcare worker. What's her name…? Noelene. She hinted the murders might have been committed by a serial killer."

Dusty recounted to Jack what Noelene Hyett had said to us outside Pearl's Shell.

"That reminds me," said Jack. "I found out something about her. Nothing to do with the case though."

"Tell us anyway, Jack."

"The poor woman was a victim of an attempted rape when she was only thirteen. She was on her way home from school one afternoon when a car pulled up beside her. A man jumped out, grabbed her and bundled her into the boot of his car."

"Serious? Thirteen years old! She must have been terrified."

"Attempted rape? Did she manage to escape?" I asked.

Jack nodded. "Her abductor drove out to a deserted area and dragged her from the boot. Luckily, he was disturbed by a couple of hikers. He jumped back in his car and sped away. The police never caught him."

Dusty exhaled deeply. "Poor Noelene. Even though she escaped being raped, it was a terrifying experience for a thirteen-year-old to go through." An admiring quality entered her voice as she continued. "You'd never guess something like that had happened to her. She seems like such a strong person."

"Good for her," said Jack. "You think she knows something about the murders?"

Dusty lifted her cup of hot tea. "Not sure. I wondered if she was trying to tell me something. Being a local means she's in a good position to pick up on what's happening around here. Perhaps she's heard something. Or she might have knowledge without being aware of it."

Dusty picked up her mobile phone. "Noelene offered to help us. Now's her chance. I'll text her and arrange a meeting."

When she'd sent the text Dusty gave Noelene's details to Jack. "See what else you can find out about her. There could be a link in her life to lead us to a killer. I wouldn't be surprised if she knows him, even if she doesn't know he's a murderer. Sean and I will talk to her and see what we can get straight from the horse's mouth."

A short time later Dusty's phone pinged with a message. She glanced at it and grinned at me. "Or maybe the camel's mouth." The mischievous gleam in her eye caused me to suspect some sort of trickery was afoot.

"How would you like to visit a camel farm?"

"I wouldn't."

Dusty chuckled. "Come on. Your affectionate friend Sindbad might be there."

I looked at her through narrowed eyes. She laughed and gestured at my Akubra which I'd placed on the empty seat next to me.

"You'd better hang on to your precious hat this time."

"Very funny." I grabbed my hat and dropped it onto my head.

Still laughing, Dusty picked up her handbag.

"I'll sit here for a bit," said Jack. "Afterwards, I'll snoop around town; see what I can find out. Catch up with you back at the shack later." I wondered what the owners of the luxury beach house where we were staying would say to their accommodation being referred to as a shack.

Dusty retrieved the car keys from her bag and tossed them to me.

"Why are we going to a camel farm?" I said as I followed her out to the car.

"That's where Noelene is."

I was bending down to unlock the car, which we'd parked in the shade of trees at the back of the cafe, when we heard shouts coming from across the road.

"Someone's in trouble!" I followed Dusty as she raced over to the bus stop.

"Leave me alone, Jimmy!" A pregnant woman in her twenties was wrestling with a man around the same age who was intent on taking her bag. The purple streak in her hair sparked my memory. It was the same woman I'd seen on the stairs at Pearl's Shell. The man was significantly taller than her. A bulging pot belly added to his bulk.

"Gimme the bloody money, you cow!"

"No! I need to buy food for the kids."

The man raised his arm, fist clenched to strike. As usual, with her advanced karate training, Dusty acted before I had a chance to even think about it. She ran forward and blocked the striking arm with lightning speed.

"Leave her alone," she hissed.

The man peered down at her like a mastiff inspecting a toy poodle. "Who the bloody hell are you?" he sneered. "The peewee from Pesky Creek?"

That's when I saw Dusty's feet move into an open stance. Unfortunately for him, the six-foot-two bully didn't notice. Before he knew what was happening, he was on the ground.

I took out my phone and called the police.

The woman stared down at the man who was struggling to escape. Dusty had one of his arms pinned to the ground with her leg while her body pressed against his back.

To my surprise, the woman started screaming at Dusty.

"Leave him alone. You stupid cow!" Cow seemed to be a favourite insult with these two.

Dusty, flushed but barely out of breath, swivelled her head around to look at the woman. "You want me to let this creep go? Is that what you want? Let him get up to bash your head in?"

"None of your business," snarled the woman.

"Yeah," grunted the trapped bully, trying to lift his face off the ground. "None of your bloody business. She's my woman."

"Fine!" Dusty released her hold on the man and jumped up. Her victim clambered to his feet and slithered a safe distance away. Dusty used her phone to snap a photo of him. I guessed she wanted evidence for the police in case he disappeared before they arrived.

The man directed his attention at the woman. I positioned myself to block any approach he might make toward her.

"Let's get out of here!" His hands curled into fists again but he checked himself after a sidelong glance at Dusty.

"I'm going to buy food for the kids," said the woman. Police sirens in the distance alerted the man. He ran. The woman turned on Dusty again. "Who gave you the right to stick your nose in? Why don't you mind your own business?"

Dusty's nostrils flared. "It is my business – it's everyone's business." Her eyes flicked from the woman to the retreating back of the man who was now turning the corner at the end of the street. "If you let him abuse you, your sons will think it's okay to abuse women; your daughters will think they have to let men abuse them." Dusty locked eyes with the woman. "This is not the first time he's hit you, is it? I bet you have bruises under the long sleeves of your top."

Subjected to the merciless stare of Dusty Kent, the woman's bravado evaporated although she remained defiant.

"What d'ya want me to do?" I heard a tinge of helplessness in her tone. "Jimmy's my husband; the father of my kids."

A bus rounded the corner and approached the stop.

Dusty sighed. "And when he's not in a rage he's a good man and he really loves you and adores the kids." The bus pulled in with a screech of brakes.

"Exactly." The woman turned her back to Dusty and boarded the bus. The doors hissed shut and the vehicle pulled away.

Dusty and I were left to explain to the uniformed police officer, a tall, thickset man with bushy black eyebrows who seemed to know Jimmy and his 'woman' although he refrained from revealing anything about the pair.

"What happened?" Jack arrived as the police car was pulling away.

When we recounted the incident to Jack, she reproached Dusty for lecturing the unfortunate victim.

"You know how difficult it is for a woman to remove herself from an abusive relationship, especially if she has children. Don't you think you were a bit hard on her?"

"It made me mad the way she let rip at me after I'd done my best to protect her."

"Why do you think she did that, Kent? She was scared, that's why."

"Scared?" I said. "This was *after* Dusty stopped her low-life husband from beating her up."

Jack adopted the tone of a patient teacher. "She was scared because after being humiliated by a woman half his size and thwarted in his attempt to beat his wife, Jimmy is bound to take it out on her later, in the privacy of their home. And that beating will be worse than anything he might have done in the street."

Dusty's face blanched. "Shit!" She turned a pleading look on Jack. "I couldn't stand by and let him punch her in the face, could I?"

Jack reached out and squeezed Dusty's arm. "No, you couldn't. Hopefully *no-one* would walk by and let some cowardly excuse for a man beat up a woman in the street. That's the dilemma. When we intervene, there's a risk the woman will suffer even more later on. I'm not saying it's what will happen, I'm just saying it's a possibility." Determination panned across Jack's face. "In fact, I'm going to make sure it doesn't happen."

"How?"

Jack didn't answer. "Send me the photo you took of the charming Jimmy." She strode toward her borrowed Volkswagen Beetle with an air of single-minded purpose.

Dusty called after her. "Jack! Be careful."

"I'll go with her." Dusty made to join me but I urged her not to. "It might inflame things if Jimmy sees you, assuming that's where Jack's going."

I soon discovered Jack hadn't set off to find Jimmy. When I slid into the passenger seat next to her, surprised at the generous leg room in the Beetle, the look on her face brooked no conversation. The silence prevailed for the journey into the town centre where she parked outside the sports bar of a pub in Dampier Terrace.

The motorcycles parked up against the verandah rail sparked my interest and caused me to realise how much I missed my Triumph Thunderbird which I'd left behind in Melbourne. Each of the tables under the verandah was occupied by a single male, each dressed in a T-Shirt and shorts. Some were busy on their mobile phones while others gazed with vacant expressions out at the ocean. Jack pushed open the door to the bar and marched inside, barking out a command to me as the doors closed behind her.

"Stay here!"

I obeyed, but glass panels allowed me a view of what was going on.

Jack approached two men who might have been members of a bikie gang judging by their tattooed muscles and aggressive beards. They listened to Jack, their faces serious. When she finished, they looked at each other for consensus before giving Jack the thumbs-up. Jack held out her phone. I assumed she was showing them the picture of Jimmy texted through by Dusty.

Jack's satisfaction was evident in the broad grin on her face when she rejoined me outside. "Done and dusted." She slapped her palms across each other. "Don't ask," she warned when I opened my mouth to speak.

On the short drive back to where Dusty's car was parked, Jack seemed about to open a window into her life, perhaps as a reward for my silent obedience.

"I was married once," she said.

As a barman, I'd developed good listening skills. I'd also acquired a sixth sense about the nature of the confidence a bar patron was about to share with me. Now, my barman's intuition warned me Jack's tale would be a distressing one.

Jack, it seemed, heard intuitive warning bells of her own. After pausing to look at me, she said, "I might tell you about it one day."

Even as the tension eased out of my body, a barb of guilt admonished me for my selfishness in not wanting to share the burden of this woman's story. Jack, however, did not seem to take it amiss. When we reached our destination, she swung her car in beside Dusty who was leaning up against the boot of her Holden.

"It's all good, Kent," said Jack with a grin. "Thanks for the loan of your bodyguard."

She left us to carry out her 'snooping' while Dusty and I set forth for the camel farm, my hat stowed on the back seat.

# CHAPTER 21

Following Noelene's directions, we travelled along Cable Beach Road, turned right into Gubinge Road and eventually turned onto Gantheaume Road bordered by deep red earth. The isolated camel farm looked to be a dry and barren place. Camels grazing on the sparse greenery along the driveway were unconcerned as Dusty's car passed them. I brought the car to a stop in front of a cluster of sheds. I had intended to leave my hat stowed in the back seat. The strong sun changed my mind.

The sense of isolation was exacerbated when we found no-one in attendance in the sheds. A table cluttered with used mugs and documents in one corner of the first shed probably served as a workspace as well as a dining table.

"Looks like they have their official office somewhere else," said Dusty.

I agreed. "This must only be a place for the camels, like horse stables."

We wandered outside again and went around to the back. The occasional bellowing of camels I'd noticed in the background earlier became more pronounced. Beyond the sheds we could see some of the humped animals grouped together in dusty fenced paddocks with drinking troughs under shade canopies. Some of them, perhaps curious about the human visitors, had approached the fences. They stood with their noses high in the air, apparently sniffing for new scents but looking as though they were viewing us with haughty insolence.

Dusty pointed at two figures next to a camel in the shade of a solitary tree in the paddock closest to the shed area. One of the figures, dressed in jeans and a blue shirt, turned and beckoned us when Dusty called out. As we drew near, I recognised her as Noelene. An older woman in a pair of camo cargo shorts that came to below her knees was caressing the neck of the camel. The short sleeves of her mustard-coloured top revealed heavily tattooed arms. Greying hair combed back from her face and pushed behind her ears might have been a futile attempt to achieve a modern slicked back look. Her eyes, I noticed when she shot a furtive glance in our direction, were washed out pools of vacuity, the colour of faded denim. This was Muriel Brown, the woman who'd been across the street with Noelene the day we visited Pearl's Shell.

When Noelene introduced us, Muriel accepted our handshakes while she studied our feet. These two women seemed unlikely friends. Noelene was confident and well groomed. Muriel, with her tentative manner and downcast eyes, gave the impression of someone who was used to living on the fringes of society.

"This is Benji." Noelene gestured at the camel.

Now Muriel came to life. Her expression brightened. "Isn't he beautiful?"

The camel bent his long neck and nuzzled her. He wasn't as big as Sindbad, but I was careful to keep my distance in case he had a similar mercurial nature.

"A camel's an unusual pet," said Dusty, after a meaningful glance at my Akubra.

"Not for me," said Muriel.

"Brownie's a camel handler," explained Noelene. "She works part time on the sunset camel tours."

"Oh, yes. Sean and I went on a camel ride on Tuesday." Dusty kept a straight face and thankfully refrained from mentioning my camel adventure. Instead, she steered the conversation to what we'd come to talk about.

"Noelene, I appreciate your willingness to help me with the case I'm working on." Muriel cast a sly glance at her friend but she nodded as if she assumed Dusty was also addressing her. "I'd like to talk to you about Petra Venter."

"Like the police?" Muriel stroked Benji's neck, keeping her eyes focused on the dusty earth.

Noelene laughed. "The police asked us about Petra." She gave her friend's arm a reassuring pat. "I tried to explain to Brownie the police treat everyone like suspects, even friends of the victim."

Dusty smiled at Muriel. "I'm an investigative journalist not a police interrogator."

"It was awful what happened to Petra," said Noelene. "And the other two women. Do you think the three murders are connected?"

"I honestly don't know, Noelene. But when I saw you the other day outside Pearl's Shell, you suggested the murders might have been committed by a serial killer." When Dusty said this, I was sure I detected a faint smirk on Muriel's face. The woman was beginning to make me feel uncomfortable.

"Was there any particular reason you thought that?" said Dusty.

Noelene shook her head. "It seemed an obvious explanation, that's all. But it's probably just me trying to play detective." She laughed deprecatingly. "My fertile imagination. I watch too many crime shows."

I could see Dusty wasn't convinced. "Did you hear something, or see something which made you think the same person was responsible for all the murders? It could be something you're not even aware of yourself."

Noelene's brow furrowed. "Something in my subconscious, you mean? That's possible, I suppose. How can I retrieve it?"

Dusty reassured her. "It might come to you when you least expect it. Whatever it is, please contact me. It might help me find who killed your friend."

"I will." Noelene's expression became serious. "The person who murdered these women must be caught."

"I agree," said Dusty. "Fern's death has to be my primary goal, but I cannot ignore the other two victims, especially as they were killed in the same spot. My investigation will include Petra and the third victim, Vicki French."

"Thank you." Noelene tugged on her friend's arm. "Did you hear that, Brownie?"

In answer to Noelene's question, Muriel turned toward us and smiled. It was a broad smile which seemed out of place on her face, as if she wasn't used to moving her lips to that extent. Then she resumed patting the camel's back.

Flies, which no doubt hung out with the camels, had scented new blood and swarmed over to offer me an unwelcome greeting. I waved them away with my hat. They returned almost immediately to settle on the same exposed areas of my skin.

Noticing my discomfort, Noelene gestured to a log shaded by the tree and covered with a large saddle blanket, brightly patterned in Middle Eastern style.

"The flies are attracted to the drops of perspiration on your face." She flicked a hand at a couple of the insects hovering near her. "If we sit over there, you might cool down a bit. No point going up to the sheds; they're not air-conditioned."

# CHAPTER 22

"**T**ELL ME AS much as you can about Petra," said Dusty when we were settled on the log. It was surprisingly comfortable. Muriel remained standing, leaning against the flank of Benji. Why don't the damn flies swarm all over him instead of giving me grief?

"Petra worked at Forrest Road Early Learning Centre with you, Noelene," said Dusty. "Is that right?"

Noelene took her phone out of her pocket. "I'll show you a picture of her." When she had the image on the screen she held it up for us. We were looking at an attractive woman in her late twenties with a round face, green eyes and a pert nose. With her simple yellow dress and vivacious smile, Petra was the epitome of fresh youthfulness. Her shining eyes and direct look suggested she was confidently anticipating any delights life might offer.

"Gorgeous hair."

Dusty was acknowledging a fellow redhead. Petra's long hair was a carroty red rather than the auburn red of Dusty's, but her hair was the same crinkly style. Its striking colour and wild mass created an eye catching natural headdress.

"Looks like the photo was taken at the Early Learning Centre," I said.

Petra was standing under a bright blue archway which appeared to be part of a children's playground.

"It was," said Noelene. "But Petra and I weren't just colleagues. We would often hang out together. And Brownie too, didn't you, Brownie?" Muriel agreed with a slight movement of her head.

Noelene swiped the screen. "Here's one of the three of us on a night out."

This image showed Petra looking stunning in a red dress. Standing next to her was Noelene in a sleeveless black dress that fell to just above her knee and accentuated her body shape. Muriel appeared to have made only a minimal effort to smarten her appearance.

"The three of us would go out together sometimes. Around to the pub or to Diamond Box," said Noelene.

The trio seemed to be a dubious match as friends. Although on second thoughts I realised, Muriel was the mismatch with the other two women. It wasn't only that she was older; her appearance and demeanour also set her apart. Next to Petra and Noelene, she faded into the background as though she had been inadvertently caught in the shot and belonged in a different group of people.

"After she split up with her boyfriend, Petra and I were saving to go overseas together. We both wanted to get out of Broome."

Muriel lowered her eyes. Was she hurt because she hadn't been included in the trip? On the other hand, she might have been asked but couldn't afford it.

"What a shame Petra's no longer here to enjoy travelling with you," said Dusty. "Are you still going?"

"I've already resigned from work."

"Resigned?"

A broad smile brightened Noelene's face. "This is the big trip; travelling around Europe for a few years."

"Noley won the lottery."

Noelene shot her friend a disapproving glance. I guessed she did not want her win to be public knowledge. Muriel caught the look and bit her lower lip, apparently aware she'd let slip something she shouldn't have. However, Noelene recovered her composure quickly.

"Brownie makes it sound grander than what it is." She laughed. "I did win some money on Lotto but not enough to put me in the world's richest people list. My win happened not long after Petra died." Noelene's face clouded over. "I lost interest in the trip after that. It was always something Petra and I were going to do together. It wouldn't be the same without her."

"What made you reconsider?"

Noelene and Muriel exchanged smiles. "Brownie agreed to come with me. We decided we'd go to the places Petra had wanted to see; go on her behalf sort of thing." Apparently embarrassed at her sentimentality, a pink tinge crept up Noelene's neck. She gave Dusty and me a pleading look. "I'd really appreciate it if you kept it to yourself. Brownie and I are the only people who know about my win. I'd like to keep it under wraps for the time being."

"Understandable," said Dusty. "There's no need for me to mention it."

I gave my assurance as well. Dusty returned to an earlier comment of Noelene's.

"You said Petra broke up with her boyfriend. When was that?"

"They split up a few months before she died," said Noelene.

"Greg," added Muriel.

"Yeah, Greg Birch. He's a wildlife photographer."

"How did he react to her death?"

"Not well. He was pretty much besotted with Petra." Noelene paused. "It made him a bit too controlling."

Dusty leaned toward her, alerted by something in Noelene's voice. "How do you mean?"

"I dunno. A few things Petra said. For example, he didn't like her going out with her girlfriends, wanted to be with her all the time. When he was away on a job he'd text or call her several times a day. I think that's why she broke it off in the end; she found the relationship too claustrophobic." Dusty's eyes met mine. Noelene had just unwittingly red flagged Greg Birch as an abusive partner. We both knew obsessed, controlling men all too often followed a trajectory in a relationship that culminated in murder. Dusty might have to reconsider her theory of a serial killer. If Greg Birch had murdered Petra, we could be looking at three different murderers.

"Does Greg live in Broome?"

"Yeah. When he's not away on location taking pictures. You could contact him through his website."

"I'll do that," said Dusty.

"I really want you to get who did this. Petra was a lovely friend, kind and generous, wasn't she, Brownie?" Muriel nodded but without enthusiasm. It occurred to me that as the odd one out in the trio, Muriel might have been jealous of the beautiful Petra.

She gave the camel's halter a tug. "I'm going to put Benji back with the herd now."

The camel turned his head slowly, considered his owner for a moment then followed her toward the gate at the end of the paddock. His progress was so slow that Muriel reached the gate long before he did and waited there.

"Is Benji sick?" asked Dusty.

Noelene laughed. "No, he's just a slow camel. Always has been. That's why Brownie called him Benji. He's named after Australia's slowest racehorse, a nag called Benji Bullet."

Muriel opened the gate and waited for Benji to go through it. Unfortunately, one of the camels in the enclosure took the opportunity to canter through the open gateway.

"Don't worry," said Noelene, as the camel lolloped toward us. "It won't hurt you. All these camels are used to humans."

To my consternation, the camel directed its attention at me. I clamped a hand over my Akubra and stepped back. At the same time, I noticed a gold name tag on the camel's halter. Sindbad! I took several more quick steps backwards. Sindbad stretched out his neck and advanced on me, his thick lower lip dropping down to expose his great yellow teeth. In Port Douglas, I'd managed to escape from a cassowary; the most dangerous bird in the world. Surely I can outrun this ungainly, big-footed creature.

Before I could make my desperate flight to safety, quick thinking Noelene came to the rescue. She picked up a couple of carrots from Muriel's bag and placed herself between us. She held a carrot out to Sindbad, gradually stepping away to keep the tempting morsel just out of his reach until she had led him back the way he'd come and through the gate into the enclosure.

Dusty and I took the opportunity to escape the camel farm after calling a quick goodbye to the two women.

During the drive back to town, Dusty slipped into a thoughtful silence. Several kilometres went by before she jerked herself up to make a startling suggestion.

"What if Greg Birch killed Petra then killed all three women to cover up the fact he'd murdered his girlfriend?"

"A bit extreme, surely?"

"You're right. I'm being foolish. It's just hard to figure out why three women were killed in this small town within weeks of each other. That's pretty extreme in itself."

# CHAPTER 23

"OH...MY...GOD!" DUSTY'S EYES were glued on a bronze sculpture about three metres tall depicting the silhouette of a naked Aboriginal girl thrusting forward through a wave, reminding me of a traditional ship's figurehead. The young girl's hands reached upward, desperately cupping a pearl shell, her hair flowing back as though pulled by water. The lower part of her body was still submerged in the wave but we could see her stomach was distended with pregnancy.

Dusty had contacted Rhona to arrange a meeting to update her on the progress of the case. Rhona had suggested meeting here in Bedford Park to introduce us to 'a pearl goddess'.

"For some reason she reminds me of Aphrodite," said Dusty.

"Me too, which is why I call her a pearl goddess. It's an apt comparison. Aphrodite is sometimes compared to a pearl because she was born fully formed and voluptuous rising out of the ocean from a pearl shell. That's exactly what a pearl does; emerges as a fully-formed finished product that doesn't need to be cut or polished."

"Aphrodite was also the goddess of fertility." Dusty inclined her head at the sculpture's expanded belly.

"Indeed. This goddess represents the women who dived for pearls."

Dusty looked at the plaque underneath. "There's no indication of her name."

"She doesn't have a name. I call her Margaret which is derived from an old Sanskrit word meaning pearl. The native language of her people, the Yawuru, might have a different name for her, but I don't know what it might be."

"Why does the sculpture depict a pregnant girl?" Dusty was gazing at the statue, her head tilted to one side.

"The pearlers considered pregnant women the best divers; they were thought to have the greatest lung capacity."

Dusty's sharp intake of breath expressed her horror. I was too shocked to speak.

"Hard to believe pregnant women were forced to dive to depths of seven fathoms for pearl shells." Rhona, whose passion for the 'gems of the moon' was today represented by a double row of large expensive looking pearls around her neck, stared out at the ocean. "I'm talking about freediving; no suits or helmets."

"It must have been a hell of a life."

"Doesn't bear thinking about," agreed Rhona. "Thank goodness those days are over. But we still have a long way to go in stopping exploitation and abuse of women."

I had no doubt Blake Montgomery was uppermost on Rhona's list of abusers.

A shout attracted our attention. We turned to see Inspector Lyons hurrying across the park toward us.

"Sorry I'm late," she said as she drew level. Dressed in a sarong skirt and T-shirt with her hair falling loosely to her shoulders, the Inspector looked more like a woman and less like a police officer today. Dusty had asked her to join us in order to give us further details of the murders of Petra and Vicki. After greeting Dusty and me and giving Rhona a warm hug, the Inspector explained she'd just arrived back in Broome this afternoon after a few days in Perth.

Dusty reassured her. "You're not late. You've arrived at exactly the right time; I was about to bring Rhona up to date with the case."

We took a respectful departure from the pearl goddess and strolled across the green lawns down to the foreshore. A picnic table provided a comfortable place to sit as well as a view of the turquoise waters of the Indian Ocean. Above us, against the backdrop of the brilliant blue sky, a flock of black kites soared effortlessly on the wind, their forked tails twisting to manipulate their flight as they searched for food on the ground below. They followed us for a short time before turning and flying back toward richer pastures in the rubbish bins of the town.

Dusty warned Rhona she hadn't been able to find any evidence to indicate Blake had murdered Fern. She stopped short of telling her Blake was almost certainly innocent because he had an alibi. Rhona's disappointment at the lack of evidence against Blake was abated somewhat when Dusty told her she would consider looking into Tiri's death after finishing with Fern's case.

Rhona closed her hand over Dusty's. "Thank you."

"We might even be able to convince the police to reopen Tiri's case," said Dusty.

Inspector Lyons looked uneasy at this suggestion; she was no doubt aware of the lengthy process involved in getting a cold case reopened. Or did she feel Dusty might be raising false hope in Rhona's heart? I knew Dusty would not do that unless she felt confident about solving the case. I wondered if she had picked up something about Blake, perhaps during our time on the *Doris*, which convinced her she could prove him guilty of murdering Tiri. If so, she hadn't said anything to me about it.

# CHAPTER 24

AFTER RHONA TOOK her leave to keep an appointment at the pearl farm, Dusty asked Inspector Lyons about Greg Birch. The Inspector dismissed any suggestion he might have murdered Petra.

"Birch was attending a wildlife photography symposium at a remote eco resort on the Kimberley coast. The only way in and out is by air using helicopters owned by the resort. He arrived there on Friday evening, was in attendance at a one day symposium all day Saturday and flew out on Sunday morning. He could not have been in Broome on the Saturday night."

"What a shame." Dusty ran a hand through her mop of auburn curls. "A potential prime suspect has slipped through my fingers."

"I can offer you a consolation prize." Inspector Lyons drew a folder from her tote bag and placed it on the table. "An infatuated male is connected to the third victim. Vicki French was a twenty-nine-year-old sales assistant at a car hire firm out at the airport; originally from Kalgoorlie, moved to Perth for work, transferred to Broome two years ago. She'd been with friends at Diamond Box Cocktail Bar but left before them, just after eleven, so was walking on her own when the killer struck."

"Is this infatuated male a jealous boyfriend?" said Dusty.

"Not a boyfriend. Apparently her manager Oliver Mayer was smitten with her. The day she was murdered he had asked her out but she declined. According to the other employees at the company her rejection put him in a dark mood for the rest of the day. Initially, when we interviewed him, he was evasive about his movements the night of Vicki's death. When we pressed him, he admitted to following her that evening." The Inspector paused. "I think he followed Vicki on a regular basis. Mayer says he returned home around nine o'clock and stayed in after that. A neighbour reported seeing his car pulling into the driveway around nine."

"But *did* he stay in?"

"He says he was playing an online chess game most of the evening with another player in Kenya. We haven't been able to contact his chess partner. The authorities in Kenya haven't got back to us as yet."

"But you didn't seriously consider him as Vicki's killer?"

"No. The frangipani motif links the murders of Vicki and Petra. If we accept that Mayer murdered Vicki because she rejected him, we'd have to assume the same motive for his killing Petra. We found no evidence Mayer showed any interest in Petra, let alone asked her out."

The Inspector sorted through the papers in her folder, retrieved several photos and spread them across the table. Each photograph showed a close-up section of a woman's neck. "The strongest link between the second two victims is the imprint from the ligature left on their throats." She tapped one of the photos to draw our attention to the image. It was a distinctive star pattern. She placed one more photo in front of us. "This is an image of Fern's neck. The ligature mark is a simple thin line without any pattern."

Dusty studied the images. "May I keep these?"

"Certainly. You're welcome to take the folder with the notes also. If need be, you can come into the station and peruse the full files relating to the case. Let me know. I'll be in Broome for several more weeks."

"Being here must remind you of your time with the water police."

The Inspector stared at the ocean. "I loved being out on the water all the time."

"You've done well since those days," said Dusty. "I understand you were one of the youngest women in this state to achieve the rank of inspector."

Inspector Lyons nodded absently. Her attention was still on the ocean as if it had stirred fond memories.

"What about your colleague, Senior Sergeant Thorn?"

"Spike?" The Inspector's voice had a nostalgic quality to it. "Spike and I…" She laughed and tossed her head back, her hair catching the sun as she did so. "Here I am reminiscing about old times when I should be helping you. Where were we?"

Dusty let her question about Thorn go unanswered. She was really fishing for more information as I had earlier updated her on what I'd found out about Thorn. He was now Detective Superintendent Thorn, based in Perth and married with three children. However, according to someone on a police online forum, he had been a 'chick magnet'. I found a photo of him, tall, rugged and freckle-faced, in a police gazette taken on the occasion of his promotion to Detective Superintendent.

When I showed it to Dusty she said, "I can see why he might have been a chick magnet. It's the eyes and the crooked smile."

Since then I'd discovered something else I hadn't had a chance to report to Dusty.

"Want to hear something juicy?" I said after Inspector Lyons had left.

"I'm all ears." Dusty flashed her familiar cheeky grin.

"Senior Sergeant Thorn was holding a torch, as my grandmother would say, for Tiri Welsh."

"Serious? Did he even know Tiri Welsh?"

"He did. He was assigned temporary security duty to Tiri and Blake during a charity event in Broome and he was invited to the after party. Apparently, Tiri was quite taken with him. She paid him a lot of attention. He was 'starry eyed' about her."

"Understandable," said Dusty. "A provincial cop meets one of the world's most beautiful women. Bound to have an impact on him."

# CHAPTER 25

LATE AFTERNOON THE next day, Dusty and I strolled across an immaculate lawn surrounded by swaying palms on our way to meet Oliver Mayer. The park overlooked the Indian Ocean across which the sun would later set. The day had been warm and humid but now a sea breeze lowered the temperature by a couple of degrees.

Dusty pointed to a group of people up ahead. "Looks like our meeting place."

As we drew near we could see a chess match was in progress. Sixty-four black and white tiles had been set in the paving to create a giant permanent chessboard. The polyurethane plastic pieces were each around a metre high.

Both players looked to be in their sixties. I watched as the 'white' player walked across the tiled squares to slide a pawn to a neighbouring square with a casual swipe of his foot. The man at the other end stood in reflection, stroking his chin as he considered his next move.

Park benches and rocky ledges provided seating for spectators. We had no trouble recognising Oliver Mayer. Inspector Lyons had described him as serious looking, early forties with short dark hair, probably wearing black clothes. When Mayer suggested Dusty meet him here, he had told her he'd be sitting at the 'black end' of the chess set, under the boab tree.

"On the rock ledge, in the black T-shirt and jeans," said Dusty when she spotted him.

Mayer was sitting alone on the surrounding ledge which, being higher, provided a better view of the chess game than the park benches where most people were seated. We skirted the playing area, approached him and introduced ourselves. He looked up at us with a hesitant smile. His was a weak face, I thought; not the sort of face I expected the manager of a car hire agency to have. But was it the sort of face a killer might have? Dusty had taught me enough about murderers for me to know it was futile to try to answer that question. I did wonder about his eyes though. They seemed to be veiled as if he was trying to stop others from looking through 'the windows to the soul'.

Dusty sat down next to Mayer. I leaned up against the trunk of the boab tree where I could hear their conversation while observing the players.

Mayer told us watching chess games here was a regular after-work pastime for him.

"I play chess a lot. Usually online," he said, with an insipid smile. "Here in the park, I just like to watch. The way the players behave is almost as entertaining as the game. Some people take it seriously and get quite emotional. Others are just plain funny."

Dusty chatted with him briefly before Mayer turned his attention to the chess game. At that point, Dusty was alerted to an incoming text message from Jack. After reading it, she held it out in front of me. *Where are you? Have info re Oliver Mayer.* Jack had promised to find out what she could about Mayer 'on the street'. Dusty texted back asking Jack to meet her in the park cafe. Jack responded: *Be there in five.*

When the chess players paused again to contemplate their moves, Dusty suggested to Mayer that he continue watching the game and meet us in the cafe when it was over.

Oliver shrugged. "I don't need to stay to the end. Sometimes the game doesn't finish anyway. The players leave when they've had enough."

"No worries," said Dusty. "Shall we say half an hour?"

He gestured his agreement with a wave of his hand, his attention already back on the game.

Dusty and I adjourned to the pleasantly air-conditioned cafe we had passed on the way to the chess area. Our wine, along with a tray of assorted nibbles including olives, nuts and cheese had just arrived when Jack breezed through the door, breathless from rushing and possibly the excitement of what she had found out. She was wearing her 'man' outfit minus the baseball cap and reflector sunglasses which had been pushed into the back pocket of her shorts. Dusty pushed the glass of beer she'd ordered for Jack across the table.

"Catch your breath. Have a drink. Then talk."

"Got the goss on Vicki's boss," Jack said when her breathing was back to normal. "Thought you'd like to know before you spoke to him."

Dusty raised her eyebrows. "You think he has potential as a murderer?"

"Could be. Your Inspector Lyons told you Vicki turned him down when he asked her out on the day she was murdered, but it's worse than that."

Dusty straightened, her interest piqued. "What do you mean?"

"Apparently, so the story goes, Mayer had been out to lunch with some important clients, consuming plenty of good food and wine. He came back with enough Dutch courage to ask Vicki if she'd like to go out for a drink with him that evening. Not only did she turn him down; she laughed. Not because she was being derisive. She genuinely thought he was joking. When he asked her, he had a huge grin on his face. To hide his nervousness or to try to look cool or some such. He ended up looking more like a clown. As a result, Vicki thought he was only fooling around. Mayer was deeply offended when she laughed at him."

"Would Vicki have accepted his invitation if she'd thought he was serious?"

"No. Apart from not being attracted to him, he was her boss. It was against company rules for staff to 'fraternise and fornicate'."

"Fraternise and fornicate?"

Jack grinned. "Not the terminology used by the company but that's what it comes down to. Why not call a spade a spade, eh? And get this. Vicki also told one of her workmates she had sometimes experienced the sensation of being followed."

"That fits with what the Inspector told us," said Dusty. "She thinks Mayer was in the habit of following Vicki."

A knowing expression crossed Jack's face. "Fits the pattern. Unrequited love. Stalking is the only way they can feel close to their heart's desire. Stalkers often become intimidating in order to exert control over their victims. They can become murderers. Especially if they've suffered a humiliating rejection." Dusty pushed the tray of olives closer to Jack who hadn't yet had anything to eat. "And what's more, Mayer's stalking was creepy." Jack put up a hand to decline the olives.

"Creepy? How so?"

"He wore a disguise." The hint of a smile played on Jack's lips. "He dressed as a woman."

"You mean he's a cross dresser?"

"Not according to my sources. He didn't actually wear a dress. He wore bits and pieces to make people think they were looking at a woman; a wig and women's shoes and clothes which weren't too gender specific – jeans and a bright coloured top."

"Smart," I said, remembering how Jack used props such as a bulky watch to convey the impression she was a man.

"You're a super sleuth, my clever friend." Dusty held up her right hand to exchange a high five with Jack. "Good work."

"No worries, Kent. Looks like I've handed you a prime suspect on a plate."

Jack drained the rest of her beer and stood up.

Dusty protested. "Stay. Have something to eat."

"Nah. Don't wanna spoil my appetite. Meeting a couple of contacts for dinner soon. Might be able to learn some more useful gossip."

# CHAPTER 26

"HAVE YOU LIVED in Broome all your life?" Dusty began with a conversational gambit when Oliver Mayer joined us a short time later.

"Nope." Mayer slipped a cube of cheese into his mouth. Prompted by our silence following his monosyllabic answer, he elaborated. "My mother and I moved here when I was fifteen."

He paused to order a glass of white wine from the hovering waitress; a smiling teenager wearing a black short-sleeved shirt and her hair pulled back from her face.

"You're virtually a local," said Dusty with a grin. "Where were you before coming to Broome?"

"Fitzroy Crossing." Mayer reached for the wine the waiter had placed before him.

Since arriving in Australia, I'd travelled the continent on my motor bike. I remembered Fitzroy Crossing because of its isolation more than anything else.

"A tiny town in the Kimberley region," I said.

"In the middle of nowhere." Mayer pulled a face. "My parents ran a roadhouse there. That's where I started playing chess. Nothing else to do, really. I couldn't wait to get out of the place when my father died."

"Broome's pretty isolated too," said Dusty.

"At least there's a beach."

"What about your mother? Does she feel isolated here?"

"Mum died a few months ago. Cancer."

"Please accept my condolences. Were you with your mother when she passed away?"

Oliver Mayer's bowed head nodded. "She was in the hospital but I was with her when she went. I didn't want her to be alone."

Dusty leaned forward with a characteristic gleam in her eye which reminded me, as it often had in the past, of a cat lining up her prey. She'd possibly noted Mayer's similarity to Dr Shipman who was also with his mother when she died of cancer. Perhaps uncomfortable under Dusty's scrutiny, Mayer changed the subject. "I live in the house on my own now. I thought I would be lonely, but it's okay."

"Are you divorced?"

Mayer shook his head. "Never been married. Had a few girlfriends, but…" He paused. "I dunno. Never met the right one, I suppose."

In other words, he wasn't comfortable when it came to relationships.

"You've done well in your job." Dusty was edging her way toward what she wanted to talk about.

He beamed. "Worked my way up from the bottom. Now I'm the manager." His tone of voice revealed his pride in his accomplishment.

"Vicki French was one of the employees you were in charge of?"

"We worked as a team," corrected Mayer.

"Fair enough." Dusty looked directly at him. "According to the police you followed Vicki the night she was murdered."

Mayer averted his gaze.

"Were you worried about her safety? Did you think she might be in danger?"

Dusty knew this was not the reason he'd been following Vicki, but she wanted to hear his explanation for herself.

Oliver Mayer hesitated. Was he considering using Dusty's suggestion as an excuse? Eventually, he shook his head.

"Were you fond of her?"

Mayer said nothing.

"On the day Vicki was murdered, I understand you asked her out and she declined."

"You win some; you lose some." His flippant tone didn't deceive Dusty.

"You must have been disappointed though?"

"Of course. But it is what it is; that's what I reckon."

"Being rejected by someone you care about can be hard to accept. It hurts, doesn't it? In particular when that person laughs at you."

Mayer clenched his jaw but didn't respond.

"You might have wanted to hurt Vicki the way she hurt you, to get back at her."

Mayer shifted in his seat and pushed his empty wine glass away.

"You followed her that night, didn't you? You were dressed as a woman, weren't you?"

He jerked his head in surprise.

"Why did you follow her? Did you want to hurt Vicki, Oliver?" Dusty's voice was low and coaxing. He glared at her. "Did you catch up to her, hit her over the head and strangle her?"

Oliver Mayer pushed his chair back and stood up, a vein in his neck pulsating. "You're talking rubbish!"

Dusty looked after him as he marched out the door. "What do you think? Can you see him sneaking up on a defenceless woman in a dark alley and knocking her over the head?" I had to admit it wasn't difficult to imagine Oliver Mayer doing that.

"Me too," said Dusty. "He's in his forties, never moved out of home and is not good with relationships. Maybe his mother dominated him, made him feel powerless. She died right before the murders started. Her death could have been the trigger."

"Maybe he'd always suppressed a desire to have power over her."

Dusty pointed her index finger at me in approval. "Quite possible. Women who thwart him, who block his wishes by rejecting him, as Vicki did, could represent his mother. His sense of frustration and impotence as a result of Vicki's rejection led to a compelling need to assert his dominance. Murdering her was his way of exerting power over her."

"Right." I sipped the last of my red wine. "Sounds like an open and shut case."

Dusty ignored my jest. "I'd have to reconsider my serial killer theory. If he killed Vicki because she rejected him on the day she was murdered, he's hardly likely to have murdered the other two women to throw suspicion away from himself since he wouldn't have known he was going to kill Vicki."

"What if Mayer had also been rejected by the other two victims?"

Dusty's eyes appraised me. "An interesting suggestion." I was chuffed at her approval. "It's possible he knew Petra," Dusty mused. "What about Fern? I doubt they would have moved in the same social circles."

"He runs the hire car joint at the airport. Fern must have been out to the airport from time to time. Right? Could even have hired a car from Mayer."

Dusty's eyes gleamed. "Good point. All we have to do is find the evidence. If I had proof he'd been rejected by Fern and Petra as well as Vicki, I could use it to put pressure on him."

"Or you could just trick him into confessing."

"Trick? Moi?" Dusty affected an expression of injured innocence, belying the fact her clever use of words to trick suspects into thinking the game was up had been effective in the past.

# CHAPTER 27

"MAYBE WE CAN find out something about the Satanist group this evening, Sean."

It was the following Monday. I'd discovered an Irish pub in town complete with Guinness on tap and pool tables. Back home in Castlerea, I'd been a champion pool player and I liked to keep my hand in. This evening I had tempted Dusty, who enjoyed anything that presented a puzzle, to join me with the promise of a quiz night.

Over the weekend Jack had gathered 'some intelligence on Muriel and Noelene' including a rumour suggesting Muriel belonged to a secret group in Broome that practised Satanism. Dusty was ready to dismiss this as small town gossip.

"On the other hand," she had said, "maybe Noelene has suspicions about that group, or someone Muriel knows in the group; someone she suspects of being a killer. That could be what she was trying to tell me when she hinted at a serial killer in Broome."

Earlier this evening, Jack had left the beach house on what she referred to as an undercover surveillance job. She hadn't given us any details.

Judging by the number of people in the pub, trivia night was popular. On a small stage, a three-piece Irish trio comprising a violinist, a guitarist and an accordion player, enhanced the atmosphere with traditional music. All the tables were occupied with people clapping to the beat. They erupted into enthusiastic cheers when the trio finished their lively rendition of a miner's song. The trivia master took the stage, brandishing a sheet of paper with prepared questions.

Dusty and I leaned against the bar to watch the proceedings, me with a glass of Guinness, Dusty with a gin and tonic.

"Doesn't look like any spare chairs so I guess we can't join in." Dusty pulled a long face.

As I scanned the room, looking for a table which might be short on players, a waving hand attracted my attention. Noelene Hyett had spotted us.

"Why don't you join our team?" she said, when we approached the table. "We could use a couple of extra brains."

Muriel was sitting next to Noelene. Seated opposite was a woman in her mid-thirties with long blonde hair and next to her, two men of similar age in navy T-shirts. At the other end of the table, with a score sheet and a pen, sat the trivia team leader. It was Oliver Mayer. He acknowledged us with a curt nod, lowering his eyes quickly before returning his attention to the score sheet in front of him.

Noelene introduced the team as The Snubfin Snobs. "We're not really snobs; it sorta went with snubfin and we didn't want to call ourselves The Snubfin Dolphins."

Someone managed to find two extra chairs. With a little jostling, room was made for Dusty and me at the table.

"Petra used to come sometimes."

Muriel's random observation piqued my interest. It meant Oliver Mayer had a link to two of the murder victims: Petra and Vicki.

I had no time to contemplate this further as interval was over and the quiz was in full swing again. Dusty answered several questions by leaning toward Mayer and speaking sotto voce to prevent players at other tables from overhearing. I thought I might have a chance of contributing if questions about Ireland or the UK were included. Unfortunately for me, the focus was mostly on Australia.

The quizmaster delivered his first question in a booming voice. "What year did the Australian constitution come into effect?"

Several people at our table responded at the same time in hissed whispers. "1901!"

Oliver Mayer marked the answer on the score sheet. I had been keeping a keen eye on Mayer and noticed he cast surreptitious glances at Dusty during the game. I fancied I detected fear in his eyes.

"What is the term given to a four wheel drive that has only been driven in an inner-city suburb?"

The blonde woman on our team was quick off the mark. "Toorak Tractor!"

"Which former Australian Prime Minister once received a pair of budgie smugglers from Broome Surf Life Saving Club?"

"Tony Abbott!" Everyone at our table seemed to know that one.

I missed the next couple of questions while I pondered the term 'budgie smugglers'. I'd heard the expression before but never quite understood it and hadn't got around to looking it up on the internet. A gift offered to a Prime Minister by a surf club? A unique pair of sunglasses? I came out of my reverie just in time to hear a question I knew the answer to.

"What's the most venomous snake in Australia?"

"Taipan!" I hissed.

The T-shirted Australian man across the table grinned and stuck his thumb at me in approval. "Handy thing to know in Australia, mate."

"Now for our final question," said the quizmaster. "Are you ready?"

"Yes!" A loud chorus from the room.

"Which religion is associated with the practice of sticking pins into a doll in order to cause harm to someone?"

"Voodoo!" Muriel spat out her answer with the excited confidence of one who knows without a doubt they have answered correctly.

Later, when the answers to the questions were given out, confirming she was correct, Muriel clapped her hands and bounced up and down in her seat grinning. Although the team on our table had a high percentage of accurate answers, it wasn't quite enough to win the prize. No-one appeared to mind very much. Their aim seemed to be on having fun rather than winning the prize.

When Noelene noticed a friend sitting at the bar and went over to her, Dusty seized the opportunity to talk to Muriel.

"You were pretty snappy with the voodoo answer. Do you know a lot about that sort of thing?"

"Everybody knows about voodoo and sticking pins in dolls."

"What about Satanism?" Dusty studied Muriel.

"Satan is an evil spirit." An all knowing smirk drifted across Muriel's face, suggesting she knew more than she was letting on. Her smirk sent a shudder of unease through me just as it had at the camel farm. Dusty didn't seem to have experienced the same negative reaction, but Muriel's comment about Satan had aroused her interest.

"Do you belong to a Satanist group?"

Muriel's eyes swivelled sideways at Noelene who had just returned to the table.

"Do I belong to the Satanists, Noley?"

"Come on Brownie," said Noelene, slipping into a vacant chair. "Confess your sins."

Muriel giggled.

Noelene turned to Dusty. "Brownie's a black witch."

Muriel's giggles increased.

"At least, that's what some people in this parochial hamlet say." Noelene rolled her eyes. "Brownie doesn't care. She thinks it's a badge of honour to be considered a black witch, don't you Brownie?"

Muriel grinned her agreement, her pale eyes shining.

"People in small towns don't have enough excitement in their lives so they make up fantastic things about people." I detected the hint of a sneer in Noelene's voice. "Anyone who's a bit different is fair game for their warped imaginations. Just because Brownie likes dragons and unicorns and fairies, they assume she believes in all things supernatural or evil." She fixed her dark eyes on me. "It's like saying someone who believes in leprechauns is a devil worshipper."

"Right." I acknowledged her point. I'd grown up around people who believed in leprechauns and I'd accepted that belief as merely another facet of everyday life. I would never have linked it to anything evil but people who didn't understand might do so.

"Good point," agreed Dusty. "I apologise, Muriel. I didn't mean to imply you were evil. I'm afraid I have to ask awkward questions to drill down to the truth. Along the way I dig up a lot of extraneous information that often has to be discarded."

"It's okay," said Muriel. "I don't mind."

With his head bowed and without a word, Oliver Mayer slipped away. Instead of going up to the bar as I expected, he kept on walking toward the exit, picking up his pace as he neared the door.

"I don't mind what you ask me either," said Noelene, "if it helps you get to the truth about what happened to Petra."

Dusty was never one to miss a cue. "Actually, there was something I wanted to ask you."

"Fire away."

"Did you see Petra the night she was murdered?"

I thought I saw a brief flash of wariness in Noelene's eyes. Dusty might have noticed it too because she hastened to clarify her question.

"You and Petra and Muriel often went out together. Did you meet up with her that evening?"

"Oh, I see what you mean. We didn't even know Petra was working at Diamond Box that night, did we Brownie?" Noelene didn't wait for her friend to answer, but Muriel shook her head to indicate her agreement. "Brownie and I had our regular Friday evening pizza at my place."

When the conversation was interrupted by the others on the trivia team calling out to Dusty and asking her about her books, I took the opportunity to decamp to the pool tables.

# CHAPTER 28

On the walk home later, I reached for my phone then remembered I'd left it on the bench by the coffee machine. I was keen to see if an email from Los Angeles, an email that could hold the key to this case, had come in.

A few days ago, Dusty had asked me to see what I could dig up on Blake Montgomery. After extensive searching on the internet, I'd found a link between him and a guy called David Lopez in Los Angeles which I thought might lead me to a drug connection. I hadn't been able to find out much on my own so I'd reached out to a couple of contacts in the States. One of them eventually got back to me. He indicated it looked like a very interesting story but he needed more time to get the full details. His email could arrive any day. I hadn't said anything to Dusty about it as yet in case it turned out to be a false alarm.

"What are you looking so glum about? And don't walk so fast." Dusty was having difficulty keeping up with me. It didn't take much for my long legs to out stride her. My desire to get back to the beach house as soon as possible must have quickened my pace.

"Not glum," I lied, shortening my stride to allow her to catch up. "Just puzzling over one of the trivia questions. What on earth is a budgie smuggler?"

Dusty looked perplexed but her expression cleared as realisation dawned. "Oh, yeah, I remember." Her eyes gleamed with mischief. "You know budgie is short for budgerigars, don't you?"

"I do. But we're not talking about illegal smuggling of parrots, are we?"

Dusty chuckled. "No, we're not. We're talking about men's

stretchy bathers. Imagine a budgerigar fast asleep wrapped in a piece of stretchy material. That's basically what you see when you look at a guy wearing a pair of these skimpy bathers, when you look at him front on. Looks like he's got a budgie stuffed down his pants."

"Strange gift to give to the Prime Minister of Australia."

"Not really. The whole country knows Prime Minister Tony Abbott, now ex-Prime Minister, wears budgie smugglers when he goes for his morning swim." I struggled to visualise other male world leaders in tight-fitting skimpy bathers.

"You can never have too many budgie smugglers." A grin spread across Dusty's face.

It was after eleven when we arrived back at the beach house which was in darkness.

"Looks like Jack's not home yet," said Dusty as we let ourselves in. "I'd better open a window for Spratt to get out."

I hurried over to the coffee machine and picked up my phone. To my disappointment, the email I was waiting for had not come through. When Dusty returned I had a pot of coffee brewing.

"He was on the window sill peering longingly at his tree," she said, sliding onto a stool across from me.

I had not yet asked Dusty about her mother and thought this might be a good opportunity. However, my phone vibrated and distracted her.

"That reminds me," she said, reaching for her phone. "Jack might have sent me a message." When she looked up from the screen, she was smiling. "A text from Jack. I must have missed it when it came through earlier. Believe it or not I haven't checked my phone since breakfast."

I raised my eyebrows in disbelief.

"It's true! I've been busy with other stuff." She held her phone up. "Look! Jack sent this at 12.18pm."

"Proof you haven't checked your phone since lunch time. Since breakfast is stretching the facts."

Dusty poked her tongue out at me and scanned Jack's text. "She says, according to the bush telegraph, there's a new lady in Blake

Montgomery's life. Her message isn't very clear; she's hopeless at texting."

"She might have discovered the Broome Satanists."

"Possible. I'll call her. No, that's no good. Her phone's always on silent and tucked away out of sight when she's working so she won't answer anyway. Never mind, I'll get the full story from her when she gets back here."

Dusty's voice had faded into the background as I checked my phone. A new email had arrived. I could hardly contain my excitement. The information that had come in from the United States was dynamite.

"If it's a story you want," I said with a grin, "then have I got a story for you!"

Dusty stopped in the act of slipping her sandals off and looked up at me.

"You look like you've found a million dollars," she said. "Tell me!"

"A couple of years ago, Blake Montgomery tried to kill a man called David Lopez."

"Serious?" With her eyes still fixed on me, Dusty let her sandals drop to the floor with a soft splat.

I gloated inwardly at her reaction. "He shot at Lopez with a semi-automatic pistol." I was enjoying myself, pacing the delivery of the information for optimum effect. The next piece of news was sure to surprise her even more.

"He'd just found out his daughter Cindy was not his biological child."

"Serious? This Lopez dude was the father?"

"Correct."

"Blake's daughter is fifteen years old. And he only found out he wasn't the father a few years ago. Really?"

I pointed at the screen of my phone. "That's what my contact in Los Angeles is saying."

"Tell me, tell me! What happened?" Dusty leaned toward me in anticipation. I told her how before they were married, Blake and Fern sometimes spent their weekends in a cabin at Big Bear Lake about two hours drive from Los Angeles. Lopez and his wife lived in a cabin on a neighbouring property. By the time of the shooting incident, Blake had sold his cabin. He had bought the *Doris* as a wedding present for Fern. Any time they wanted to get away, they went on the yacht. Lopez, on the other hand, was still living at Big Bear Lake.

On the day of the shooting, according to Lopez, Blake Montgomery marched onto his property, red in the face with anger, brandishing a gun and threatening to kill Lopez who tried to escape out the back door. Blake went after him and started shooting. Lopez ran as fast as he could in a zigzag pattern to avoid being shot. At some point, he tripped and fell. Blake stood over him with the gun pointed at his head. When I reached this part of the story, Dusty broke in with an exclamation of astonishment.

"Holy Nelly!"

"Fortunately for Lopez," I said, "Blake had run out of ammunition."

"Very fortunate. The shooting can't have been reported in the press at the time or the whole world would have heard about it."

"Right. Lopez didn't press charges against Blake. In fact, the incident wasn't even reported to the police. It seems only Montgomery and Lopez knew. It surfaced last year because Lopez had consumed a few too many drinks at his wife's funeral and started shooting his mouth off."

"Hm. So until then he'd kept quiet about what happened to prevent his wife from finding out." A cheeky grin preceded Dusty's next remark. "Or maybe he was afraid of his mother-in-law." She became serious again. "It seems the charming Blake Montgomery is capable of committing murder when his temper is up. I think I'd better double check his alibi for Fern's murder." Dusty paused to sip her coffee. "So how did Blake find out he wasn't his daughter's biological father?"

"Cindy, with the help of her grandparents in Wales and without the knowledge of her mother and father, was delving into family history. The idea was to have a full family tree done as a surprise for her parents."

"A surprise all right." Dusty grinned.

"Right. Anyway, in the process of her family research, Cindy had a DNA test done. The results indicated her father was Latino. When she recovered from the shock she asked her parents about it."

Dusty's eyes widened. "I would've liked to have been a fly on the wall for that discussion."

# CHAPTER 29

WE'D FINISHED BREAKFAST and I was on my second cup of coffee the next morning when Dusty jumped up and ran down to Jack's room. She hurried back to grab her phone.

"Jack didn't come home last night." She dialled her friend's number and put the phone to her ear, pacing up and down while waiting for Jack to pick up. When she didn't get an answer, she dialled again, pacing more vigorously now. Finally, she gave up, removing the phone from her ear.

"Why doesn't she answer?"

Dropping the phone on the table, she stared at it as if willing it to ring. "Something's happened to her, Sean." She ran her hands through her hair, causing her mop of wild curls to look unkempt. "Something's happened to Jack." Her eyes pleaded with me to prove her wrong.

I didn't know Jack very well but I knew she would not have left Spratt to his own devices without letting Dusty know. I also knew better than to offer Dusty reassuring platitudes. She needed something practical.

"Come on." I pushed back my chair. "Let's go and see what we can find out."

A car door slammed outside.

"Jack!" Dusty rushed out through the open doorway to greet her friend. However, it wasn't Jack walking along the path. It was Inspector Lyons.

"Matilda!" Dusty ran forward and grabbed her hand. "Jack's disappeared."

The Inspector's smile faded. A shadow flashed across her face before she regained her composure. Dusty was so worried about Jack I don't think she noticed. I wondered what it was about Jack disappearing that bothered Inspector Lyons. Did she know something that might be relevant?

"Please help me find her," said Dusty.

"Of course." Inspector Lyons placed a gentle hand on Dusty's arm and steered her back into the house.

"Take a few deep breaths," she urged, coaxing Dusty into one of the chairs at the dining table and sitting down next to her. "Now tell me what's happened."

I swung into action preparing fresh coffee. Dusty explained the situation to Inspector Lyons. The Inspector took her phone from her belt holster, asked Dusty for a description of Jack and called the police station. Dusty and I listened to her one-sided conversation with the officer-in-charge. The Inspector's expressionless face gave nothing away. When she finished, she placed a reassuring hand on Dusty's arm.

"There's nothing to suggest anything has happened to your friend. A patrol car has gone out to do a thorough search of the streets. They'll also check with the hospital." She poured a mug of coffee from the pot and nudged it close to Dusty. "In the meantime, I'll fill you in on the details of Wasim Smith's alibi." While she was speaking she poured out two more mugs of coffee, pushing one across to me. I observed the ease with which she took charge. It came as second nature to her.

"What do you mean?" Dusty raised one eyebrow and tilted her head at Inspector Lyons.

"Wasim Smith's alibi checks out exactly as he said. He was talking to a passing stranger on the boardwalk outside his friend's yacht until around midnight."

"How come this passing stranger didn't come forward before?" Dusty sounded suspicious. She might have thought Wasim had arranged for someone he knew to contact the police and claim to be the stranger.

"The man left Broome the following morning working as crew on one of the yachts and has been out at sea for several months. He wasn't aware WAPOL wanted to speak with him. The sailor only found out we wished to speak to him when he telephoned a friend in Broome. The friend told him about the murders and happened to mention the police were looking for a witness who had been on the marina that night. The sailor got in touch with us immediately."

I could see Dusty was not ready to accept Wasim's innocence but she said nothing.

"There has been a further development," said the Inspector. Dusty brightened, perhaps anticipating a piece of evidence to confirm another suspect. She was disappointed on that score.

"We've received another note from the killer with a frangipani enclosed." Inspector Lyons paused. She had our full attention but seemed hesitant about divulging the information.

Dusty prompted her. "What did it say?"

The Inspector, sombre faced, retrieved a piece of paper from a folder. "The actual note was on a thick piece of white paper that looked like the side of a carry bag, the type used for transporting takeaway food. We believe it was retrieved from a rubbish bin. We've checked CCTV from the main shopping strip but it looks like the killer chose a bin without cameras in the vicinity. This is a copy of the note."

The message had been composed with letters cut from a magazine or newspaper and stuck onto the white paper.

The message read: *I have the power to kill again. Killing is thrilling.*

My stomach tightened into a nauseating crunch when I read the last line. Dusty was similarly affected. Her face blanched. "Jack! Oh, no. He's got Jack, hasn't he?"

I realised the significance of Inspector Lyons's earlier consternation when Dusty had told her Jack was missing. She must have guessed then that the killer had Jack. However, she allowed none of that to show now, seeking only to reassure Dusty.

"We can't jump to conclusions. Didn't you tell me your friend has been tracking suspects and watching criminals for many years? She knows how to stay out of trouble, doesn't she?"

Dusty agreed but did not look appeased.

I offered what I thought might be reassurance. "Jack might have been following someone and wanted to stay on their tail all night for some reason."

Hope flickered in Dusty's eyes but died quickly. "She would still have responded to my messages."

"You said she always keeps her phone on silent and out of sight when she's on the job. If she was up all night following someone, she might have fallen asleep somewhere without checking her messages."

Dusty's half smile suggested she wasn't convinced.

The Inspector's phone trilled. We all tensed. News of Jack. Was it good news?

"Is it the station?"

Inspector Lyons answered Dusty's question with a brief nod after glancing at her phone. Perhaps anticipating bad news, she rose from her chair and moved away to take the call.

Across from me, Dusty sat with both hands clasping her mug, eyes squeezed shut. When she finished her conversation, Inspector Lyons turned back to us. She shook her head as her eyes met mine over Dusty's head. "No news of Jack, I'm afraid." Her tone of voice indicated she had more to say. Picking up on this, Dusty opened her eyes. She relaxed her grip on the coffee mug and turned to look at the Inspector.

"It's Blake Montgomery," said Inspector Lyons. "He's been reported missing. His yacht is not at the marina."

# CHAPTER 30

"WHAT DO YOU mean? Missing?" said Dusty. "He's probably gone cruising on the ocean."

"Mr Montgomery had a couple of appointments yesterday which he missed. According to his PA, it's not like him. She's been unable to contact him on his mobile. At first she assumed he was simply out of range but when he missed his appointment with her and another with the local mayor, she became concerned. When the yacht failed to return last night, she contacted us at the station. The coastguard has been unable to raise a response from the yacht and they cannot locate it."

"Curious. He seems to be evading contact. Do you know when he left the marina?"

"The *Doris* was seen heading out to sea around eleven yesterday morning."

I recalled how Dusty and I helped Blake launch the yacht the day we went out with him.

"He must have someone with him like," I said. "He wouldn't be able to get the yacht out safely on his own."

Inspector Lyons looked thoughtful. "I think I'd better have a word with his assistant." When Dusty reached for her bag, obviously planning to accompany her, the Inspector smiled. "You can tag along if you want."

"We want," said Dusty.

At Dusty's insistence, I sat in the front seat. "You'll need room for your long legs," she said as she clambered into the back seat of the Inspector's car.

During the drive, the significance of Jack and Blake disappearing at the same time dawned on Dusty. "Jack was following Blake. What if she's out there on the ocean with him? What does that mean? If he's deliberately staying out of contact and he's got Jack…" Her eyes opened wide. She clamped a hand across her mouth. I couldn't think of anything to say to calm Dusty as she continued her fearful speculations. "Did she find out something which incriminates him in Fern's murder? Has he taken her out to sea to throw her overboard? My god! She could disappear without a trace."

The Inspector locked eyes with Dusty in the rear-view mirror. "Calm yourself. We don't even know he's got Jack."

Dusty's eyes scanned the passing landscape as though she hoped to see Jack out there. When she turned her attention back to the driver's seat she wore a worried expression. "Matilda, do you think Blake Montgomery is dangerous?"

The Inspector kept her eyes on the road ahead while she considered Dusty's question. In her agitated state, Dusty rushed on with more questions.

"Did you know Blake and Tiri? What was he like? Do you think he could be dangerous?"

The Inspector answered without turning her head. "The only time I met Mr Montgomery when he was married to Tiri Welsh was at a fund-raising dinner. I was part of the security team assigned to protect them for the evening."

"Why did they need protecting?"

"The dinner was to raise money to build a world class cyclone proof marina in Broome. Boating facilities here at the time were rather primitive. Just the same, some locals objected to the building of a marina. One or two of them had been vigorous in their objections, even threatening violence."

Dusty's interest had been piqued, temporarily overshadowing her concerns about Jack. "Did you notice any strain in their relationship that evening? How did Blake seem with Tiri?"

"Patient."

It wasn't the answer I'd expected. Dusty also seemed surprised.

"Patient? Did Blake have cause to be patient with Tiri?"

"The woman's dead and it's not relevant anymore." Something in the Inspector's tone suggested she might be persuaded to elaborate despite her respect for the deceased. Dusty was always quick to pick up on every nuance in an individual's voice. Today was no different.

"It's not something I need to publish in my book. I'm asking out of personal interest really. So far I've only heard glowing, and no doubt glorified, reports of Tiri. You might have observed something which could give me a fuller picture of her as a human being."

Dusty waited in silence while Inspector Lyons came to terms with her conscience. After a few moments, as she executed a left hand turn from the main road, the Inspector responded.

"All right. I'd heard rumours Tiri was an incorrigible flirt. That evening I saw it for myself. She wasn't interested in the men she flirted with; it was a display of power. She knew she could have any man she wanted and took pleasure in making it plain to everyone around her. It didn't matter if the man was a dishwasher, a gardener, or an executive; she'd give her special treatment to the most desirable looking man in her orbit until he was putty in her hands. Underneath her charm and practised sincerity, I'm sure she was gloating inside."

"One of *those* women." Dusty nodded her understanding. "Who was her target at the fund raising dinner?"

"My sergeant. Spike. Senior Sergeant Thorn." I detected an edge of bitterness in the Inspector's tone. "He wasn't exceptionally handsome but he had the invisible something which makes some men irresistible to women."

"The X factor," said Dusty. "Also known as the SEX factor."

"Yes. Tiri Welsh spotted it straight away. She made a beeline for him." The Inspector's jaw clenched. "But she was only using him."

"You mean they had an affair?"

"No. She just led Spike on enough to let him think he had a chance. He became besotted with her." Inspector Lyons shook her head in distaste. "I knew her game. She was using Spike to provoke jealousy in her husband."

"Talking about jealousy," Dusty continued, "what do you think happened on the *Tooting Moon* that night? Do you think Blake assaulted his wife and threw her overboard?"

"I don't know. I know she knew how to push his buttons. I think she enjoyed making him jealous. It's possible she was playing one of her manipulative games and went too far."

"When you found her in the water, she was already dead. Correct?"

The Inspector's hands tightened on the steering wheel as she recounted what happened. "I caught a glimpse of her red sarong in the water, dived in and swam out to it. When I got there it was only the sarong."

"No sign of Tiri?"

"None. Spike had a spotlight from the boat shining on the water. He moved it across the surface. That's when I found her. She was floating in the water nearby. I hadn't seen her in the dark."

Dusty leaned forward, a gleam in her eyes. "What did you do?"

"I put her in the rescue hold and got her to the boat as fast as I could."

Mindful of the Inspector's regret in not saving Tiri's life, Dusty didn't pursue the subject. She sat back in her seat and remained silent for the rest of the drive. I guessed her thoughts had returned to Jack.

# CHAPTER 31

At Kayla Bassett's streamlined, clinically clean office in Hammersley Street, the Personal Assistant welcomed us with an air of expectation, assuming we had news of Blake. Inspector Lyons quickly disabused her of that notion.

"I just require more information to try to ascertain when Mr Montgomery left and why."

Kayla shook her head. "I don't know why he left. He's never done anything like this before. I'm worried."

"Who helps him launch the yacht when he takes it out on his own?" I asked.

"I do." Kayla beamed. "I help him with the slip ropes and act as look-out until he's clear of the dock. The rest he manages himself."

"You didn't help him on this occasion?" said Dusty.

"I had no idea he was taking the *Doris* out. The marina staff must have helped him."

The Inspector took over. "Ms Bassett, I need to be absolutely sure whether we have a problem here. A full scale search would take a significant amount of police time and resources. Are you sure your boss hasn't simply gone off for some quiet time on his own? After all, he has been under a lot of pressure in the past few months."

Kayla's eyes whipped the Inspector. "Thanks to you! It wasn't enough that he was grieving for his wife. You had to accuse him of murdering her as well."

Inspector Lyons's expression remained impassive. She must have become hardened to these sorts of outbursts from members of the public over the years. Her next question was delivered in a cool, authoritarian tone.

"Do you know why he might be trying to stay out of contact with everyone?"

Kayla, her mouth set in a hard line, shook her head.

"Do you have any reason to believe Mr Montgomery could be in an unstable frame of mind?"

"Wouldn't you be after going through what he's been through?" snapped Kayla.

"I'll take that as a yes," was Inspector Lyons's droll response. "Since you have given me reason to believe he might be a danger to himself, I'll authorise a search for the *Doris*." Striding toward the door, she took out her phone and began dialling. "I'll be in touch as soon as I know anything," she called over her shoulder.

"Thank you," said Kayla, her anger now dissipated. "I'm sorry. I should have offered you a cup of coffee." The Inspector was already out the door and didn't hear the belated offer but Dusty seized on it.

"We would love some coffee, if it's not too much trouble. There's a few things I need to talk to you about."

At a glance from Dusty, I hurried outside to let Inspector Lyons know we'd make our own way back. When I returned, Dusty and Kayla were seated at the table, now cleared of the papers that had been there earlier. The aroma of coffee permeated the small office.

"Mr Montgomery found it difficult to continue writing his memoirs after his wife died," Kayla was saying. "He kept putting it off. In particular, he avoided writing the section about Tiri Welsh's death. At one stage I suggested a counsellor could help him work through it. He gave me such a glare I backed off."

"An insult to his manhood," suggested Dusty.

"I think that's the way he saw it." Kayla pulled the coffee pot toward her and deftly poured the hot liquid into three mugs. "If your friend is on the yacht with Mr Montgomery, she won't be in any danger." Dusty must have shared with Kayla her fears about Jack being on the yacht. Kayla passed a mug of coffee to Dusty and slid one across the table to me as she continued. "I doubt she's with him. If he's gone away to have a few days to himself, he wouldn't take anyone, least of all someone he doesn't know."

"I hope you're right," said Dusty, glancing at the screen of her phone which she'd placed on the table. She didn't want to miss any calls or texts lest Jack tried to get in touch.

"Actually, Kayla, it looks like Blake chose a different way to get through his writer's block." Despite her concern for Jack, Dusty was not going to pass up on the opportunity to find out whatever she could from Blake's PA.

Kayla looked at Dusty, her expression a mixture of suspicion and curiosity.

"I received a text from Jack yesterday. In it, she suggested Blake has a new lady in his life."

The colour drained from Kayla's face. "So it's true," she murmured as though to herself. Her shoulders sagged. "I saw him with a dark-haired woman the other day, at a restaurant." She pressed her lips together, staring down at her feet as she confronted the destruction of her illusions about winning the heart of 'Mr Montgomery'.

Dusty pounced on her vulnerability. "Kayla, why did you lie to me the other day?"

I was sure this was a shot in the dark. Although Dusty sensed Kayla had lied about something, she didn't know what. Her question was phrased to give the impression she knew more than she did. This strategy had worked for her in the past. It caused the interviewee to respond on the assumption Dusty already knew the truth.

Several expressions relayed across Kayla's face: surprise, shame, guilt, chagrin.

Dusty persisted. "It's time for the truth."

Kayla struggled to keep her emotions from showing but she couldn't prevent the trembling of her lower lip.

Dusty was merciless. She fixed her eyes on the PA in a stare I've seen her use before. It's a look that seems to bore deep into the victim's psyche. Mere mortals cannot resist its power and invariably offer up the secret they were desperate to hide. That's exactly what Kayla did.

"I didn't lie, not really." Her jutting chin expressed defiance. "I did go to the yacht to look for Mr Montgomery's handwritten notes."

"But?"

"It was the evening before. Not the night his wife was killed."

"I see. So Fern was out that evening as well. You must have been aware she used to sneak out to meet her lover when Blake was asleep." It was obvious Kayla spent time spying on Blake but Dusty spared her the embarrassment of having to admit it.

"Thank you for telling me. I realise you were motivated by a desire to protect your boss." Dusty's voice was gentle now, her tone sympathetic. Behind the ruthless interrogator Dusty became when determined to elicit the truth from someone, was a compassionate heart.

"Do you know who the woman is?" she asked. "The dark-haired woman you saw Blake with at the restaurant."

Kayla shook her head. "I took a photo through the window. With my phone. I've never done anything like that before. I was so scared Mr Montgomery would turn around and see me. I snapped the shot and ran. Such a stupid thing to do." Tears brimmed in her eyes.

"Nothing stupid about it." Dusty's dismissive tone was designed to lessen Kayla's embarrassment. "People do it all the time, take photos of other people in public places. You're too hard on yourself." A slight smile of gratitude played across the PA's lips. "In fact, you've done us a great service. We need to find this woman to check whether she's on the yacht with Blake. May I see the photo you took?"

Kayla reached into the side pocket of her bag to retrieve her phone. When she had the image on the screen she held it up for us to see.

An involuntary *Ah* escaped my lips. The face looked familiar to me but I couldn't place the woman.

"Do you know who she is, Sean?"

"I think I've seen her somewhere."

Dusty suggested various options. "At the pub on quiz night? Walking along the marina? At Pearl's Shell?"

A memory stirred. "I think I saw her face on an advertising board or something of the kind."

"Relax. Enjoy your coffee. That way, your subconscious might kick in and tell you where you saw her face." Dusty turned to Kayla. "Thank you for being so helpful." Her voice was gentle but Dusty wasn't finished with the PA yet. "Is there anything you can tell me which could be useful? Even something apparently insignificant to you could become important later on. For instance, is there anything about Fern that might be relevant?"

Kayla considered this for a moment before answering. "She did have a stalker last year."

"A stalker!"

I was as surprised as Dusty. This was something that hadn't been mentioned in the police file.

"Do you know that stalking is often a precursor to murder? This guy could be the killer." Dusty threw her arms in the air. "I don't understand why you or Blake didn't mention him."

"Not that kind of stalker. It wasn't a man. It was a woman; just a pathetic woman who wanted to be close to someone famous. When Mr Montgomery confronted her, she was very apologetic and promised to stop. He did intend to report her, but Fern felt sorry for her. She said the woman was harmless. Anyway, the silly woman stopped the stalking after she was spoken to. After that, we forgot about it."

"Did you find out who she was?"

"Her name is in the files." Kayla got up, went over to her desk at the other end of the room and clicked open a folder on her laptop. After a few moments, she looked across at us. "Found it." She tore a pink sheet from a pad of sticky notes, wrote the name on it and returned to her desk. "Her name is Brown." She handed the note to Dusty. "Muriel Brown."

# CHAPTER 32

"MURIEL BROWN. CAN'T say I'm surprised," said Dusty. "I can see Muriel following someone famous because she wanted to feel a part of their world."

After taking our leave of Kayla, we had decided to stroll into Chinatown, a few minutes away, for an early lunch.

Dusty looked up at me, her head to one side, a thoughtful expression on her face. "What if Muriel was jealous of Fern? Jealousy can provoke unexpected violent responses."

"You mean she was jealous because Fern had everything: beauty, money, a handsome husband, an adoring public and all that sort of stuff."

"Exactly! All that sort of stuff can make other women super jealous. But, if I'm honest, I see Muriel more as an adoring admirer than a killer." She paused. "On the other hand, some other woman might have been jealous enough to commit murder."

"Who? Shama? Noelene?"

"Neither of them has a motive. They are both attractive and too self assured to become obsessed with jealousy. But there is one woman who could be a green-eyed monster."

"There is?"

"Yep. Kayla Bassett. Something about her seems not quite right. I reckon she's hiding something. She's obsessed with Blake; that much is clear. What lies behind the facade of our organised and efficient PA?"

"An organised and efficient killer who commits murder to protect the object of her obsession from a woman unworthy of him." I suggested.

"That's what I'm wondering. We know murderers are adept at hiding their dark side by presenting a likeable persona to the world."

"Like a trusted family doctor who gets away with murdering hundreds of his patients?" I was referring to a previous conversation.

Dusty pointed a finger of approval at me. "Exactly! I think it's time we, I mean you Mr Maze Master, found out more about Kayla Bassett. It makes more sense that the killer is a deranged male but you know my motto." Knowing what she was about to say, I joined in on the next sentence. "Leave no stone unturned!"

She paused in front of a weatherboard cottage almost obscured by luxuriant palms lining the fence to yet again check her phone for news of Jack. A disappointed shake of her head followed.

Dusty started to walk on when her attention was drawn to a small tree near the cottage gate. "Do you recognise this plant?" Seeing the blank expression on my face she picked a leaf from the bush. "Maybe the scent will jog your memory." She crumpled the leaf and held it under my nose.

Dusty was right. As I inhaled, the aniseed aroma brought back a memory of our time in Byron Bay. I couldn't recall the name of the tree but I remembered its oil had been the 'secret ingredient' used by a particular barman. "Espresso martini!"

Dusty laughed, thrusting a finger of approval in my direction. "That's right. Aniseed myrtle; used to add a special touch to espresso martinis."

We recalled other moments from our Byron Bay adventure as we continued walking.

When we turned into Frederick Street, I recognised it from an evening walk I had taken a couple of nights ago.

"How's your subconscious, by the way?"

It took me a second to realise Dusty was referring to her earlier remark about my subconscious helping me to remember where I'd seen a photo of the woman Kayla had observed with Blake.

"Not helpful, I'm afraid."

"Maybe she was an actor advertising a movie," suggested Dusty. "She and Blake might have met through a shared interest in acting."

I shook my head. "I think it was a local advertisement on the footpath, you know, a board outside a shop."

Strangely enough, a few seconds later, I remembered.

"Got it!" I was so pleased, I almost shouted. "It wasn't a board on the footpath. It was a sign in a window. I saw it when I was out walking the other night. I wouldn't have noticed it except the turquoise colour around the picture caught my eye and reminded me of—"

"Me!" Dusty interrupted with a grin.

"Right. It was an office front. The picture of this lady's face was part of the logo for her business."

"What sort of business?"

"She's a clinical psychologist."

"A psychologist? Interesting. The question is whether Blake was seeing her professionally or romantically. And is she on the yacht? She and Blake might be simply having a few quiet days together on their own private floating love nest." Dusty looked up at me. "Do you recall anything else about her?"

"Her name's Veronica."

"Good memory!"

I accepted the compliment without confessing to my admiration for the beautiful identical twins that are the Australian singing duo The Veronicas.

"I can't remember her last name," I admitted. "But I'm sure I can find out."

"If you saw it in this street, all we have to do is walk up and down until we find her office."

"There's an easier way." I took out my phone. With the ever-helpful search engine supplying results in my location, I soon brought up the relevant website.

"Found it! Her full name is Veronica Murdoch."

I held my mobile out to show Dusty. She dialled the phone number listed on the website. It didn't take her long to establish Veronica Murdoch was in her office. Dusty declined the secretary's offer to make an appointment and ended the call.

"Couldn't speak to her. She's with a client and has appointments for the rest of the day. At least we know she's not on the yacht."

"Why not try to speak with her about Blake?"

"I don't think she'd be very forthcoming if I asked her about her relationship with him over the phone, while she's at her work place."

"Right. Not ideal circumstances."

"What's more, if their relationship is professional, she won't give me information about a client."

"Oh my god!"

We had been walking slowly, both of us lost in thought, when Dusty's exclamation startled me. As we pulled up short, a group of tourists passed us, smiling at Dusty when she repeated her interjection and ran her fingers through her hair. Oblivious to the attention she had attracted, Dusty gripped my arm.

"What if Blake plans to suicide at the spot near Rowley Shoals where Tiri died? Maybe he's going to throw himself overboard to be with her."

"Or to bring her back."

"What do you mean?" Dusty looked nonplussed.

"Like Orpheus." I reminded her of how she'd told Blake when we were on his yacht the story of Orpheus going to Hades to bring Eurydice back from the dead. Dusty slapped her hands against her cheeks.

"You think I might have put a crazy idea in his head?"

Too late, I realised I should have kept my mouth shut. It took me a second or two to come up with a diversion.

"Your theory is he might have become unsettled by Fern's murder and the accusations that have been made against him?"

"Exactly."

"Right. In which case, if Jack is with him she won't be in any danger." No sooner were those confident words out of my mouth when a thought struck dread into me. If Blake has lost the plot and gone to Rowley Shoals, he might send Jack over the side as well. A flash of fear in Dusty's eyes suggested she had had the same thought. Damn! My big mouth again. I should have heeded my mother's often delivered advice not to dig a hole for myself.

# CHAPTER 33

When we arrived at Shady Lane Cafe in the centre of town, Dusty came to an abrupt halt at the entrance. I'd walked past her before I realised she wasn't beside me. Looking back, I saw she had retrieved her phone from her bag.

"We should talk to Muriel." Dusty was oblivious to cafe patrons politely making their way around her to get inside.

"Why Muriel?"

"I need to ask her about stalking Fern."

"Now?" The aroma of cooking meat coming from the cafe had raised my compelling desire for food to a new level. I was not going to be dragged away from the source of its satiation if I could avoid it. "Why the urgency?"

"I've got to be doing something. Can't stand this waiting; waiting to hear news about Jack, not knowing where she is or what's happened to her."

Thankfully I managed to convince Dusty to delay acting on her impulse 'to be doing something' until after we had eaten. In the cafe area, attractive wooden tables with matching chairs were shaded by a combination of leafy trees and bright yellow umbrellas. Most of the tables were already occupied. A slim young waitress in a sleeveless black t-shirt and short skirt with an order pad in her hand flashed us a welcoming smile. She pointed to a table at the back being vacated by a trio of women. I ordered a large hamburger with a bowl of chips while Dusty settled for a mixed salad.

We had finished our lunch and I was enjoying an iced fresh mango juice when Dusty pulled up Muriel's number from her contacts list, pressed dial and put the mobile to her ear.

"Muriel?"

In their brief conversation, Dusty didn't reveal to Noelene's friend what she wanted to speak with her about.

Following the directions Muriel gave Dusty over the phone, we drove to a park in Roebuck Bay and looked for what Muriel had called the bamboo corner. I drove the car along the street parallel to the park while Dusty kept her eyes peeled for anything resembling bamboo, relaying what she observed as we passed. "Barbecue area. Children's playground. Amenities block. The park looks reasonably green considering how hot it is in Broome. But I can't imagine there'd be enough water to grow bamboo."

I turned left to follow the road toward the beach.

"There it is!" Dusty pointed to a corner of the park dense with bamboo.

"Apparently they do have enough water," I said. "And some!"

"They must have tanks of grey water," mused Dusty, looking back at the striking green bamboo garden as I drove past.

After parking the car, we walked back to the grove of bamboo. We passed through the gap in the fence that served as an entry point. Dusty checked the instructions Muriel had texted. "We have to enter the grove through a tunnel." The tunnel was directly in front of us.

"Serious? Look at that. They've grown the bamboo into a natural passageway; no artificial framework or anything." Dusty was wide-eyed with wonder as we entered the green subway. I was relieved to discover it was several degrees cooler than outside. The tunnel opened out into an enclosed area furnished with man-made red and white mushrooms in various sizes, some designed for children to sit on and others large enough for adults.

Dusty turned to me and laughed. "We've come down the rabbit hole."

"Right." Unable to reach my full height and feeling awkward in a stooped posture, my level of enthusiasm did not mirror Dusty's.

Suppressed giggles came from somewhere beyond the cluster of toadstools. "Why is a raven like a writing desk?" Muriel's voice. It wasn't difficult to imagine her as the eccentric Hatter in Lewis

Carroll's story.

Dusty called out to her. "I believe I can guess that." This caused Muriel's giggles to gain momentum and erupt in a surge of muffled cackles.

Following the sound of the laughter, we came upon Muriel behind an oversized mushroom, seated at a small table set for the Mad Tea-Party. She beamed at us, clearly pleased with herself.

Dusty grinned a greeting and sat at the table across from her. After two aborted ungainly attempts I managed to perch myself on a large red mushroom.

Behind Muriel was a replica of a mirror made from some sort of transparent material. Above it a sign read: *Step through the Looking Glass.*

"Muriel." Dusty's expression became grave, signalling she had not come to play games. "This is important." A coaxing quality had crept into Dusty's voice, one she might use when speaking to a child. "I believe you were a fan of Fern Parkes."

Muriel looked up, her brows puckered in a frown.

Dusty persisted. "You admired Fern. Is that right?"

Muriel put her head to one side. "Have you guessed the riddle yet?"

Dusty was momentarily taken aback before realising Muriel was again pretending to be the Hatter. She did not allow herself to be drawn into the game.

"You used to follow Fern. Blake's Personal Assistant asked you to stop, didn't she?"

Muriel lowered her eyes as if reluctant to admit to what she'd done.

"I did stop," she mumbled.

"Did you follow Fern the night she was murdered?"

Muriel looked up, biting her lower lip. Her eyes glistened with moisture. Was she about to confess to murder? Her next words were not what I expected.

"You have brought evil here."

"You mean because I mentioned Fern's murder?"

"This is a different game, just for fun." Muriel reached into the pocket of her denim shorts for a tissue and dabbed at her eyes.

Dusty was contrite. "I'm sorry. What you say is true. This is an enchanted place of fun." She waited for Muriel to compose herself before asking the next question. "Why did you choose to meet us here?"

"I come here a lot." A sly smile slipped across Muriel's face. She pointed at the mirror. "The jabberwock lives through there. Do you want to see?" Her naive eagerness was somehow grotesque.

"I'd love to. Another time." I was thankful Dusty chose not to accept the Mad Hatter's dubious invitation.

Muriel's expression darkened. "You cannot leave here."

I turned around, half expecting our exit to be blocked by some sort of magic portal.

Dusty remained composed. "Why can't we leave?"

The Mad Hatter glared at Dusty. "You haven't guessed the riddle yet. Why is a raven like a writing desk? You said you could guess it."

"I thought I could but it's too hard," Dusty replied. "I give it up. What's the answer?"

Pleased with Dusty's response, Muriel clapped her hands. Dusty told me later her answer was a quote from Lewis Carroll's book.

"I haven't the faintest idea," Muriel said.

Giggles once again spewed from her mouth and rang in our ears as we retreated back down the tunnel.

Dusty cast an anxious glance at her phone as she hurried to the car, but there was no word from Jack or the police.

# CHAPTER 34

OVER THE NEXT few days, when she wasn't roaming the streets of Broome searching for Jack or anyone who might have seen her, Dusty paced up and down in the living area, alternating between checking her phone for messages, texting Inspector Lyons for news, and dialling Jack's number. She made sure Spratt had food and sometimes sat on the back verandah to watch him in the tree.

"He's missing Jack," she said one evening. I decided she was transferring her own emotions to the marsupial rather than making an astute observation. How could she know what emotions a sugar glider was experiencing? As she has often done in the past, Dusty answered my unspoken question.

"He's not gliding." She looked up into the tree where Spratt was perched in the fork of two branches, his tail draping below, curled at the end. "He doesn't try to catch insects; he just stares down at the ground as though he's waiting for Jack to appear."

I was doing my best to make sure that happened as soon as possible by using my 'maze master' skills to search for properties owned by Oliver Mayer where he might hide a murder victim, as well as trying to find out about Satanist groups in the Broome area. Harbouring a secret fear Jack was already dead didn't stop me from doing everything I possibly could to track her down. One morning I was lamenting my lack of success when Dusty, eyes shining, rushed into my room waving her phone.

"Blake's on his way back!" I looked up from my laptop screen. "And guess what?" She didn't wait for me to respond. "Jack's with him. She's safe! Jack's safe."

She rushed out of the room and down the stairs, calling back to me as she did so. "Come on. We're going to the marina."

Dusty was already behind the wheel of her car with the motor running by the time I closed my lap top, loped down the stairs and closed the front door after me.

"Jack's with Blake?" I scrambled into the passenger seat. "How did that happen?"

Dusty let out the clutch and pressed her foot on the accelerator almost before I'd closed the car door. "I don't know. Matilda said she received a call from Blake but the connection wasn't very clear. All she could work out was that he was on his way back to Broome and Jack was on board."

When we arrived at the marina, the *Doris* was already docking with the aid of the port staff.

Jack, engulfed in a too-large red yachting jacket, waved and shouted from the deck when she saw us. "Kent!"

The two friends collapsed into each other's arms as soon as Jack, after removing the red jacket, alighted from the yacht. She was still dressed in the black shorts and grey t-shirt she'd been wearing when we last saw her, although her fake leg tattoos had now almost faded away.

"I thought you'd been kidnapped!" Dusty stood back and gave her friend an accusatory look.

"Sorry, mate. Been offline for a few days." Jack held up her phone with a rueful grimace. "Flat battery."

"Blake could have let someone know you were with him."

"He didn't know I was on board until a few hours ago."

"What? You've been gone for almost a week!"

Jack explained she'd slipped onto the yacht unseen by Blake. While she'd been creeping around below deck trying to find anything that might help with the case, the *Doris* had left the marina without Jack realising it.

"Why didn't you send me a text before your battery died?"

"I did. I told you I was on Blake's yacht and not to worry and to look after Spratt for me. How is he? Is he okay?"

"Spratt's fine. I've been taking care of him. But I haven't received a text from you since around lunch time on Monday." Dusty pulled her phone from her bag. "Look." She opened her messages from Jack and held the phone out for her friend to see. "This is the last text I got from you; Monday lunch time at 12.18."

"That can't be right. I sent you another one immediately after that one. I realised I'd forgotten to tell you I was on the yacht in the first message." Jack looked at her own phone. "This damn thing's dead of course so I can't check. I definitely, absolutely, indubitably sent you another message after that."

"Maybe you forgot to press send," I suggested.

Jack threw her hands in the air. "Wouldn't be surprised. Done that before. And I was in a bit of a flap at the time." She gave Dusty an apologetic look. "You must have been worried."

Worried was an understatement considering the anxiety Dusty had experienced over the past few days. However, she played down the extent of her alarm.

"I was a bit worried, Jack. I kept hoping you'd run off with a bikie."

Jack clamped her hands on her hips in mock indignation. "As if!"

Blake stepped off the gangplank and paused beside us. He looked less debonair than usual although still well groomed in a polo neck grey shirt and knee length blue shorts.

"I'm on my way to the police station. Inspector Lyons wants to see me. I've been a naughty boy; taking off without telling anyone, missing appointments, creating panic resulting in a police search etc, etc." The familiar, charming grin slid across his face, easing the haggard expression. "My apologies for kidnapping Margriet." He seemed to have given Jack a new name which brought a girlish flush to her cheeks. "It wasn't intentional. If I'd known she was on board I'd have returned pronto." He made to go but turned back. "Mind you, I'm not sure I believe her reason for being on board *Doris*." He looked at his stowaway with a twinkle in his eye.

"We're going to celebrate Jack's return at Diamond Box," said Dusty. "Why don't you join us after your interview with Inspector Lyons?"

"Love to. Lunch is on me." He dismissed Dusty's objections with a wave of his hand. "It's the least I can do."

Dusty asked Jack what excuse she'd given Blake for being on his yacht.

"I told him I wanted to see what a big yacht was like because I was thinking of joining a yacht crew next year. Considering the way I was dressed," she looked down at her clothes, "I thought it might have a ring of truth to it."

"Not a loud enough ring." Dusty pointed to Blake's retreating back. "He was too smart for you."

On the walk to Diamond Box Cocktail Bar, Jack filled us in on what had happened since we last saw her.

"After I left you guys on Monday morning, I came down here to the marina. When I saw Blake leave the yacht, I took the opportunity to go on board and have a snoop around. I found a photo album with heaps of pictures of Blake and Tiri. That woman sure was beautiful. The photos told the story of their love affair, their marriage and their lives. I must have been so engrossed in the album I didn't notice the movement of the yacht."

Dusty agreed. "You do have the ability to shut everything out when you're concentrating."

Jack grinned. "All that yoga when I lived in Nimbin as a kid." She glanced at me. "My parents were hippies." Nimbin was sometimes called the hippie capital of Australia. I had visited the small 'alternative' community with Dusty a couple of years ago. "Anyway," continued Jack, "I thought Blake was just taking the yacht out for a few hours so I hid in the second bedroom at the other end of the boat."

"Before you knew it, you were trapped. A stowaway. I'm amazed you managed to escape detection for so long."

"Tell me about it! I had to be discreet about using the bathroom, just in case Blake heard the sound of the plumbing or whatever. I used to sneak into the galley and take food when he was on deck; tried to choose things that wouldn't look obvious. I was on tenterhooks the whole time expecting him to find me. Luckily, he was preoccupied with whatever was on his mind."

"And he didn't find you until this morning?"

"He didn't find me. I'd had enough of hiding and sneaking around. Also, I was afraid he might be on his way back to the United States. So I went up into the cockpit and gave myself up." Jack held her arms up above her head in the open-handed gesture of surrender.

"You weren't afraid you were turning yourself in to a killer?"

"I dunno. When I looked at the photo album and saw him and Tiri together, I kinda softened toward the man." Jack looked down at her feet, moving her right foot around in a circle before looking up at Dusty. "He adored Tiri. I could see it in his expression when he looked at her, his body language when he was standing next to her, everything." She nodded in response to Dusty's appraising glance. "I know! He could still be her killer. Anyway, coming out of hiding turned out to be a good decision, didn't it? Here I am safe and sound."

"Thank goodness. During your luxury cruise, did you discover anything useful?"

"Zilch. Definitely nothing drug related."

Dusty shrugged. "No. Sean didn't find anything to connect Blake or his yacht to the drug trade. He's innocent on that score."

"I did manage to spy on him," continued Jack. "When I heard him come below deck, I would open my door a smidge to peek out. I saw enough to know he was in a bit of a state, trying to shake off the black dog. I could see the signs. I've been there; where you feel you're in a bottomless chasm and can't get out. When I saw the state he was in this morning – gaunt face, black rings under his eyes – it was obvious he'd been going through a tough time."

"How did he react when you appeared in the wheel house?"

"Surprised. Not shocked though. It was as if he didn't care or had stopped feeling emotions."

"Interesting. By the way, how come Blake knows your name?" Dusty turned to me and explained. "Jack's real name is Margriet."

"From my Dutch grandmother."

"Such a pretty name. It's a shame you can't use it anymore."

I was intrigued by Dusty's use of 'can't'. Why couldn't Jack use her given name? Before I could satisfy my curiosity, Jack continued. "You know, most people think my name's Margaret. I have to pronounce it for them, Mahr-GREET, several times before they get it. Blake Montgomery got it right from the very first. Pretty impressive. Anyway, to answer your question, Kent, I told him my name on the way back. I thought I might get him to open up to me if I shared a bit about myself."

Dusty gave Jack the thumbs-up. "Did he divulge his intimate secrets?"

"Not exactly. He did tell me something that surprised me, though." Our arrival at Diamond Box distracted Jack. "Can't wait to have a nice cold beer."

# CHAPTER 35

WE SAT AT an outdoor table under a cafe umbrella elegantly striped in blue and white with a commodious canopy that would be the envy of a certain magical nanny.

"Have your beer later, Jack. First, we're celebrating your safe return in style." Dusty looked up at the waiter, a smiling young man with sandy coloured hair pulled back in a knot, who had materialised in front of us. His smile broadened in approval when Dusty ordered a bottle of French champagne.

"This doesn't taste as bad as I thought it would," said Jack taking a sip of the chilled champagne after we had toasted her return. "Blake's bound to have some of this on the *Doris*. She's some yacht. Can you believe he was sailing incognito? He has a special button he can press so the yacht can't be detected by any electronic means. A sort of cloaking device – like in Star Trek." Jack looked at me with a suspicious squint. "You're probably too young to know about Star Trek."

"Seen almost every episode of The Next Generation."

Jack's eyes widened in pleased surprise. "My favourite series. Don't you just love Captain Jean Luc Picard?"

Dusty interrupted our camaraderie. "Can you two save your reminiscing till later? Blake'll be here soon, Jack, and you haven't told us what it was he said that surprised you."

With a mischievous glint in her eye, Jack sipped her champagne, deliberately prolonging her answer. Dusty scowled.

"All right, Kent, I won't keep you in suspenders any longer." Jack laughed. "Believe it or not, the cultured and confident famous movie star has been seeking guidance from a psychologist. He was uncomfortable about being seen going to her office. Rumours would spread; the media would turn it into a sensational story about him going insane or some such. So he had her conduct the initial consultations over lunch and compensated her for the extra time." Observing Dusty and I exchange a knowing glance, Jack paused. "You know about this already?"

Dusty shook her head. "Not exactly. Blake's PA told us about a woman he's been meeting up with. She thought it was a new romance."

No further discussion was possible because Blake arrived, the familiar charismatic grin on his face. The black dog, as Jack called it, seemed to have left him, at least for the time being.

"Released from custody," he joked, signalling to the waiter. He ordered a scotch and, after consultation with the rest of us, a gin and tonic for Dusty, a beer for Jack and a Guinness for me.

"I apologise for the anxiety you must have suffered not knowing where Margriet was."

Dusty waved his apology aside. "It's not your fault. You didn't know she was on the yacht."

"A good skipper should know what is happening on his boat. I should have discovered her earlier. Tell the truth, I was preoccupied." He gulped down a generous serve of his scotch. "As I told Margriet," he tilted his glass at Jack giving her a warm smile. "I felt the need to be on my own. No, I suppose that's not strictly accurate. What I really felt was the need to be close to Tiri. The investigation into Fern's death stirred memories of what happened seventeen years ago. I had this sudden urge to go to Rowley Shoals – where Tiri drowned."

Was he admitting he'd gone out there to commit suicide – to die where Tiri died? If so, Jack probably saved his life. I wondered how she would feel about that if Blake turns out to be Tiri's murderer.

"Did it help?" asked Dusty.

Blake swirled the tawny liquid in his glass and stared at it for a moment, then nodded slowly. "Y'know, it did in one way. Some things became clearer to me, but…" He lifted his gaze to glance at us. "Other things got more confusing." He looked like a small boy who had received a brand new train set only to find he couldn't work out how to make the trains run. I realised how disarming his brand of charm must be to women.

"Enough of this confab." Blake picked up one of the menus on the table. "Time to eat."

"Blake," said Dusty when the waiter had taken our orders and disappeared inside. The tone of her voice should have warned Blake he was about to be ambushed but he was oblivious. "You've been keeping a dark secret."

Triumph gleamed in Dusty's eyes at the actor's startled reaction. An expression of fear mixed with guilt passed across Blake's face before he had a chance to compose himself. Dusty gave him no time to think.

"You tried to murder a man in California."

I fancied I saw a brief flash of relief in Blake's eyes before his face darkened. "David Lopez," he said, draining the rest of his scotch. He slumped back in his chair and stared out at the water. "Knowing your reputation, I guess I shouldn't be surprised you found out about that."

"Was Fern having an affair with Lopez?"

"Not an affair." Blake's lips tightened into a thin line. "I had a cabin in Big Bear Lake where Fern and I used to go to get away from the craziness of Hollywood. We went up there a couple of weeks before we were married. Lopez's property was next to ours. He invited us in for a neighbourly drink while his wife was in hospital having their first child. At some point in the evening I'd gone back to my cabin to get a bottle of Dom Pérignon to toast the arrival of Lopez's baby. I wasn't gone more than half an hour. During that time Lopez had taken advantage of Fern's inebriated state to seduce her."

"You knew nothing about it?"

Blake shook his head. "Nothing at all; not until recently when our daughter…when Cindy questioned us about the results of a DNA test she had done while tracing her family tree."

"That's when Fern told you about Lopez?"

"Yes. Until then she had no idea their encounter had resulted in conception. Finding out Lopez was Cindy's father was as much a shock for her as it was for me."

"You decided to drive to Big Bear Lake to confront him?"

"Slammed out of the house and drove straight there."

"Not before you stopped to grab a gun and ammunition."

Blake spread his hands apart in a gesture of denial. "The gun was in the trunk of the car. I had the idea of using it on Lopez during the drive to Big Bear."

"So you planned to kill this man in cold blood?"

To my surprise, Blake laughed. I detected no trace of malice or bitterness. It was more a merry chuckle, as though he was remembering a good joke.

"I sure wanted to kill him. But it would have been a stupid thing to do." He shot a meaningful look at Dusty as if to underscore the fact that he would not be foolish enough to commit murder. "I wasn't planning on killing him. The gun was loaded with blanks. It was a movie prop. It looked real. I knew Lopez wouldn't know any different. I wanted the satisfaction of scaring the jerk."

"He could have died of a heart attack from the fright."

"Y'know, I didn't think of that but I'll tell you straight up, I wouldn't have lost any sleep over it if he had."

Was that a glimpse into a cold-hearted aspect of Blake's personality? Would he be willing to cause someone's death under certain circumstances? Or was it simply a normal reaction toward the man who had cuckolded him?

The waiter arrived, excusing himself as he reached across the table with Dusty's smoked chicken salad, Jack's club sandwich, a large bowl of fresh salad and a box of hot thick chips to share. Tempted by their appetising smell, I'd already eaten a couple of the chips by the time the waiter had hurried away and returned with the meals Blake and I had ordered: two large plates each bearing a steaming grilled barramundi.

"Enjoy your meal," said the waiter as he departed.

It would have been impossible not to enjoy the superbly prepared dishes. The barramundi was sweet and succulent with a delicious buttery flavour. Dusty and Jack declared their meals equally appetising.

Towards the end of our lunch, Dusty returned to the subject of David Lopez, asking Blake how the revelation had affected his marriage. Showing no signs of irritation at Dusty prying into his personal life, he explained how he'd experienced difficulty getting over the feeling of being betrayed by Fern. Coming to terms with the knowledge his fatherhood was a lie and that Fern was the cause of it had been even harder.

"I had trouble letting it go. Y'know? That was difficult for me."

"Did it also change your relationship with your daughter," asked Dusty.

Blake shook his head. "Cindy and I have always had a strong bond." A warm smile softened his features. "I'm her dad; we adore each other. If she wanted to make contact with her biological father, I would support her but she has no desire to do so."

By the time we finished our meal, I'd 'kinda softened toward the man' to use Jack's words. I sensed Dusty had too. Had we come to know the real Blake Montgomery today? Or had he used his considerable acting ability to hoodwink us?

After paying the lunch bill and leaving a generous cash tip, Blake left us to meet up with Kayla.

"Might as well get all my apologies done in one day," he said with his familiar easy grin.

"Kayla." Dusty was pensive as she watched Blake weaving his way through the tables toward the exit. "What have you found out about her, Sean?"

"Nothing as yet, Boss." I was working on a promising lead but was not sure enough of it to say anything as yet.

# CHAPTER 36

WE LINGERED AT the table after Blake left, seduced into indolence by the warmth, the sound of the water lapping against the pylons of the pier, and the beauty of the surroundings.

After a short companionable silence, I judged the time right to ask a question which had been hovering in the back of my mind since Jack's return.

"What made you take the handle of Jack?"

A wistful expression settled on her face. It was a few moments before she spoke. "Remember I told you I was married once? I had a child and a violent husband." Satisfied with what she saw in my face, Jack continued her story, telling me how her husband had become violent and controlling after her daughter was born. With her parents living in another state and too ashamed to confide in her friends, Jack suffered in silence for several years. When she eventually summoned up the courage to face the facts, she knew she had to leave the marriage for the safety of her daughter.

"My daughter was five when I left. I didn't want to risk going to a refuge where her father could, if he tried hard enough, track us down. Anyway what sort of life is that? I also knew I'd better make a good escape. If he caught up with me, he'd kill me. I believe he would have killed our daughter as well."

The risk to her daughter would have been only too real. I recalled a recent high profile domestic violence case in Australia where a father killed his son at a public sporting event, despite the mother taking every precaution and all possible legal avenues to keep the boy safe from her abusive ex-partner.

"I saved a secret stash of money and bought an old Kombi van," continued Jack. "My daughter and I went on the road and I changed my name."

"Taking a male name was a clever strategy."

Jack agreed. "If he came looking for me it would make it a little bit harder for him to find me. I changed my daughter's name as well. She thought it was fun to choose her own name. She chose Enid after the author of *The Magic Faraway Tree*." Jack paused while the waiter replenished our water glasses. "One day, around ten years later, I found out Enid's father was in jail for killing the woman he took up with after I left. As long as he was in jail, my daughter was safe and I was free." She glanced at me. I saw the distress in her eyes. "But another woman was dead."

"Right. I can see why you were so against Blake Montgomery. I'm surprised you now seem to have changed your mind about him."

Jack responded with a half smile. "I could be wrong."

"Where is your daughter now?" I asked. "Do you see her?"

She beamed proudly. "Enid and I are close. She was on the road with me at first. Eventually, I found a safe house for her. Mum had two aunts living in a big house in Queensland. My husband knew nothing about them and would never have thought to look for us in the north. The aunts agreed to take Enid in. For her safety, I left her there." A slight tremor in Jack's voice betrayed her emotions. "Then I got out of Queensland as fast as I could."

"So that if your husband did catch up with you, it would be far away from where your daughter was."

Jack turned to gaze at the water. I sensed rather than saw the moisture she blinked away. She explained that her daughter graduated from university in Brisbane and was now a successful lawyer.

We left Diamond Box soon after that. Dusty wanted to spend some quiet time going over her notes on the case. She had lost track of where we were at over the last few days. Jack was anxious to see Spratt. I needed to get to my laptop to continue researching Kayla Bassett.

"Didn't anyone tell you it's okay to sleep in on Sunday mornings?" Dusty complained through a yawn the next day. Looking casually fresh in an island style sarong and her hair in wild disarray, she had joined me at the kitchen bench for an early morning beverage.

Pointing at the coffee grinder which I'd been using a few minutes ago she observed, "That's not the most pleasant sounding alarm clock I've ever heard."

"Sorry, Boss." I grinned at her. "But it's not exactly the crack of dawn; the sun's been up for a couple of hours. It's already raised the temperature to twenty-one degrees." Dusty accepted the mug of black coffee I passed across to her and placed her phone on the kitchen bench. No sooner had she done so than it buzzed with an incoming call.

"Matilda," she said after a glance at the screen, raising her hand to me in apology as she picked up her phone.

A few days earlier, Dusty had passed on to Inspector Lyons the information she had gleaned from Kayla about Muriel Brown stalking Fern. She felt obligated to do so, but she had been reluctant because she was concerned the woman would be traumatised by a police interrogation.

Dusty's fears were justified. Muriel Brown did cave in under police questioning. With startling results. Inspector Lyons had called to inform us Muriel had confessed to the murder of Fern Parkes as well as the murders of Petra Venter and Vicki French.

The news took me by surprise but now I had an explanation for my feelings of discomfort when I was in Muriel's presence. Had a part of me known she was a murderer? One of my aunts who had 'the second sight' was able to sense people's secrets. Maybe I had an element of that in my genes.

"Not what I was expecting." Dusty took another sip of her coffee. "Muriel seems so ineffectual. I mean, she's strange but not in an evil way. Too timid. Then again, books have been written about serial killers described as shy and introverted."

"And you weren't expecting the murderer to be a woman," I added.

"Correct. I definitely had this killer pegged as a male although I know not all serial murderers are men. I've read about female serial killers who send chills down my spine, including Rosemary West in England."

Her raised eyebrows queried my knowledge of the case. I responded with a nod. It sickened me to think of what Fred West and his wife Rosemary did to innocent young women in their 'House of Horrors' in Gloucester.

"The look on your face says it all. I agree. Just thinking of those people is nauseating." Dusty dismissed the Wests with a curl of her lip. "Let's get back to our case. I was thinking about how Noelene hinted the murders might have been done by a serial killer. Was that because she suspected Muriel? Or sensed Muriel's guilt at a subconscious level?"

"Why don't we ask her?"

"Good idea, Mr Maze Master." Dusty took her coffee with her upstairs to finish drinking it while she changed. When she reappeared a few minutes later, she was dressed in T-shirt and shorts with her hair scrunched into a frizzy ponytail.

Jack still hadn't surfaced. We left her a note before driving to Noelene's address which I'd found in the online telephone directory.

# CHAPTER 37

RESIDENTS OF ROBERT Street were lucky enough to live in a tree-lined boulevard providing extensive shade to mitigate Broome's tropical heat. Noelene's home, an attractive townhouse in white corrugated iron cladding, was also surrounded by trees. As we pulled up, Noelene closed the front door behind her and hurried down the steps. Wearing a loose summer shift with a floral design on a navy background and carrying a bag over her shoulder, she strode toward a red Toyota sedan in the carport.

"Good morning," called Dusty, opening the passenger side door of the Holden.

Noelene stopped and turned in our direction.

"Have you heard about Brownie?" she said as we walked toward her. Judging the answer from our expressions, she continued. "I'm going to the police station now. Poor Brownie; she'll need help."

"She's lucky to have a good friend like you." Dusty had, in the past, acknowledged she would not have the patience to sustain a friendship with someone she didn't find intellectually stimulating. Consequently, she admired tolerant and kind-hearted people like Noelene. "Have you got time for a quick chat? If not, I can come back later."

"It's fine. We can talk now. Brownie's not expecting me at a particular time. In fact, she doesn't know I'm going in today." Noelene walked back toward the house and ushered us into a patio area to the left of the front door. The slatted side walls of the patio and the surrounding trees provided shade and a cool place to sit. Bright green chairs and a matching table created an appealing contrast with the white of the townhouse.

"We won't keep you long," said Dusty, declining Noelene's offer of cold drinks with a flourish of her hand.

Noelene sat down and rested her bag on the patio floor next to her chair. Despite the expertly applied make-up, I noticed dark rings under her eyes. She must have spent a sleepless night worrying about her vulnerable friend.

"Tell me, Noelene, did you suspect Muriel had killed the three women? Or maybe you sensed it. Was that what gave you the idea of a serial killer?"

While Dusty was speaking, Noelene's jaw had dropped. "Brownie? You think Brownie's a serial killer?" Her tone was saturated with indignation. Her eyes were fixed on Dusty as though she were looking at a crackpot.

Never one to be intimidated, Dusty stood her ground. "It's not what I think. It's what Muriel says. Inspector Lyons told me about her confession."

Noelene shook her head. "You've met Brownie. You know what she's like. She lives in a fantasy world. Gets confused. The police probably put pressure on her. That would make her even more muddled." I admired Noelene's loyalty to her friend.

"Yes. Muriel would find it hard to cope with interrogation. But it's hard to believe police pressure impelled her to confess to murder; three murders in fact."

"Sometimes Brownie mixes up fantasy and reality. She might have thought she was playing some sort of game with the police. Or she might've told them what they wanted to hear so they'd stop harassing her. Brownie's not a killer. Any fool can see that!" The scorn in her voice surprised me. I wondered if she had a deep-seated resentment of the police from the time when she was abducted as a teenager. Did the police ill-treat her then? Did they act as though the abduction and attempted rape were her fault?

"So you believe Muriel made a false confession?"

"Of course I do. All Brownie is guilty of is stalking Fern Parkes. That's why she was taken in for questioning, you know. Apparently, someone told the cops about the time she'd been stalking Fern."

Without a trace of guilt on her face, Dusty nodded her understanding. I hoped my face was just as deadpan. "The cops put two and two together and came up with bloody twenty-two." Noelene's expression tightened. "They don't care that Brownie has an alibi for at least one of the murders. She was with me the night Fern Parkes was killed. Here." She inclined her head toward her unit. "Brownie and I were here at ten-forty-five. Actually, Brownie arrived before eight and didn't leave until almost midnight."

"Did you tell the police?"

"Of course I did. Yesterday. They weren't interested. If they bothered to interview Mrs Chi, the widow next door..." she jerked her head at the adjoining unit on the right, "she could back me up. I had to apologise to Mrs Chi the next day. She very politely suggested we had been making a lot of noise. We were watching a horror movie and got a bit carried away in the scary parts. You know, screaming and yelling." Noelene laughed self-consciously. "Anyway, Brownie's going to be assessed by the police psychiatrist. If she believes Brownie was coerced into the confession the cops'll have to let her go." She held up her right hand with two fingers crossed.

Dusty also held up crossed fingers. "So, if it wasn't Muriel, what made you think the murders were committed by a serial killer? Was it the memory of someone from your past? I apologise for bringing this up but..." The blank expression on Noelene's face forced Dusty to elaborate. "I understand you survived an attack by a vile predator when you were only thirteen." Noelene folded her arms across her chest and brought her lips together in a tight line. Dusty kept her tone gentle. "If that individual is still in the area, it's possible his behaviour has escalated to murder. I wondered if you were thinking along those lines too, a subliminal thought perhaps."

"That creep wasn't a local." Noelene's expression was grim. "I have no idea where he is now. At the time, I told myself he rolled his car because he was in such a hurry to get away and was killed. Then I forgot about him. As far as I'm concerned he's dead."

"Good. My Nan would approve." Dusty grinned at Noelene and explained. "Nan was a storyteller. She used to say we have the freedom to choose what stories we tell ourselves."

Noelene's answering smile softened her expression and eased some of the tiredness in her face. It occurred to me she might not recognise her attacker after so many years if he had returned to the area. I wondered if she believed the murders were carried out by the same killer because she'd seen him and her subconscious mind had recognised him.

Dusty, wanting to take advantage of this meeting to glean as much information as possible, adroitly distracted Noelene when she made to reach for her bag. "How long have you known Muriel?"

"Five or six years, maybe longer." Noelene relaxed back into her chair. "I met her at Pearl's Shell. Her marriage had just broken up and she needed a bit of support."

"Ah. I was wondering if Muriel was gay but I guess not."

"Neither am I, despite rumours to the contrary. Just because Brownie and I spend time together, narrow minded people in this little town assume we're a couple." Noelene rolled her eyes. "We keep each other company and have a good time when we go out together, that's all. My boyfriend's married so being seen together in public is not on. Brownie doesn't have anyone so it suits us both to hang out together."

She picked up her bag and hoisted it over her shoulder as she stood up. "I'd better go. I'm worried about Brownie."

We thanked her for her time.

"I think we should go and see Mrs Chi," said Dusty as she waved to Noelene reversing out of the driveway.

# CHAPTER 38

MRS CHI, A petite woman in her eighties with curly grey hair and large glasses, was in her front garden although she'd been hidden from view by a well established lime tree. She stopped weeding and looked up when we approached.

"Hello," said Dusty as we paused at the front gate of her cottage. The two houses were separated by a narrow strip of land on either side of a shared fence. While Noelene's home had a sleek modern look her neighbour's was an older traditional house.

Mrs Chi rose from her crouched position, removed her gardening gloves and walked toward us with surprising agility, a broad welcoming smile on her face.

"You are friends of Miss Noelene?"

Because of her name and her Asian features, I had expected her to speak with a Chinese accent but only a barely discernible twang suggested English might not be her mother tongue. Then I remembered the long history of Chinese people in Broome. Her family had no doubt been in Australia for several generations.

After we introduced ourselves and explained the reason for our visit, Dusty asked Mrs Chi about the night Fern died.

"Noelene said she and her friend were making a lot of noise that night," Dusty said, as we opened the gate and followed Mrs Chi to the shade of her front verandah. The octogenarian placed her gloves next to a wide-brimmed sun hat on the verandah rail and gestured at a vacant bench seat. I remained standing, leaning against a verandah post facing the two women.

"Those girls. Such screaming. Such yelling. I think Miss Noelene is being attacked. I must call the police. But I look out the window and nothing looks bad." Mrs Chi punctuated most of her sentences with short chuckles.

"Did you see Noelene and her friend?"

Mrs Chi shook her head. "It is enough to hear. Their noise, it keeps me awake for many hours."

"That doesn't give Muriel an alibi," said Dusty on the way back to the car after declining Mrs Chi's offer of refreshments and taking our leave. "She could have left early."

"You think Noelene lied about the time Muriel left her place?" I pressed the remote to unlock the car doors. "Would she do that?"

"I think she would; to protect Muriel." Dusty slid into the passenger seat next to me. "Maybe I'll take that up with her later." She gave me a look of mock solicitude. "Right now, you're my main concern. You must be fantasising about a big, hot breakfast."

I grinned, pulled the car away from the kerb and drove in the direction of the township. At the sidewalk cafe, during my 'big, hot breakfast' of sausages, eggs and bacon, fried beans, mushrooms and tomatoes, I reported what I had discovered about Blake's PA. I delivered my news with what I hoped was an air of nonchalance. "Kayla Bassett is not who she says she is."

Dusty's eyes shone with triumph.

"I knew it!" She clenched her fist and jerked her elbow down.

I cut a well-browned sausage in half, dipped one end into the runny egg yolk and bit it off. Dusty waited, a scowl revealing her impatience. I finished chewing the meat before continuing. "The real Kayla Bassett runs a small publishing company in London."

"Serious?"

"Serious. While I was surfing the internet looking for information on Kayla I came across an article in a UK newspaper about the London Kayla Bassett." I brought a copy of the article up on my phone and slid it across to Dusty who began to read aloud.

"*Australian publisher, Kayla Bassett, was this week awarded the best UK Independent Publisher award. Her company, Juno House, publishes books by women, for women, although not necessarily about women.*"

"At the end, you'll find a reference to her having worked with several Australian Prime Ministers, helping them write their autobiographies. If you remember, that's what Blake said about his PA."

"I remember." Dusty was studying the photo that accompanied the article. "The woman in the picture does look a bit like Blake's Kayla, minus the burgundy rimmed glasses. Maybe it's her. We don't know much about what she did before working in Broome. It makes sense that she could have been in publishing."

"Look at the date."

"Oh, I see. The award ceremony took place in January this year. Blake's Kayla was here in Broome then. She could hardly be in two places at the same time."

"I managed to extract Kayla's personal details via the website of Blake's publisher." Dusty smirked, knowing I had used my professional IT skills 'creatively'. I went on to explain I'd matched the date of birth, home address and other information with a Perth real estate agent called Zoe Austin who was the owner and sole occupier of the property listed as Kayla's home address.

"Have you found a picture of this Zoe Austin?"

"Not yet. She doesn't seem to be active on social media. Her Facebook page shows images of 'dream places to travel to' but no personal photo."

"Did you find anything to indicate Zoe Austin is dead?"

"Not as yet."

"So Blake's PA could be Zoe Austin. Why change her name?" Dusty took a sip of her tea. "Now we're getting closer to the truth. I knew Kayla was hiding something. Wouldn't be surprised if she's got a dark past."

Jack's Volkswagen Beetle pulled up at the kerb. Dusty had texted her earlier inviting her to join us. Jack's melancholy expression told us something was wrong.

"What's up?" Dusty asked as Jack slumped into a chair.

"I knew this time might come one day," she said.

Dusty and I exchanged puzzled glances. Jack enlightened us.

"Spratt's gone."

Dusty was immediately sympathetic. Not knowing what to say, I kept my mouth shut.

"He didn't come home last night. He always comes back before dawn. I'm worried he's been taken by a black kite."

We had seen flocks of the birds in the skies around Broome on several occasions.

"No!" Dusty was appalled at the idea of the diminutive sugar glider in the talons of a bird of prey.

Jack heaved a sigh. "I rescued that little fella from his dead mother's pouch. I'm the only mother he's ever known." A tear fell along one of her cheeks. She brushed it away with a rough swipe of her fist. "I never intended to keep him forever. I always wanted to return him to the wild. Sugar gliders are sociable animals. I hoped he would one day find a tribe."

"Maybe that's exactly what's happened."

Jack ran her hands through her hair, which still looked sleep dishevelled. "I need to know. Not knowing is tearing me apart."

Dusty reached across to squeeze Jack's hand. She understood the anxiety of not knowing. It was only recently that she'd found out her mother was dead after not knowing what had happened to her for almost thirty years. Jack straightened and sat up.

"Yes, Kent. That's probably what's happened. Why think the worst, eh?"

"Exactly, Jack. And thanks to clever Mr Maze Master here I've got some news to help take your mind off Spratt for a while."

"So you think Kayla Bassett might have come to Broome to reinvent herself?" said Jack when Dusty had finished.

"Well, she's not who she says she is. So who is she?"

"That is the mystery Dusty Kent must solve." Jack had regained some of her usual sparkle.

My plate was now satisfyingly empty. Jack declined my offer to order her some breakfast but accepted a cappuccino.

When Jack finished the last of her coffee she pushed back her chair. "I'm off to do a bit of snooping around."

Dusty looked alarmed. "Be careful. I don't want you disappearing again."

"No worries." Jack made a cross-like gesture over her chest. "I'll be as careful as a crocodile dentist."

# CHAPTER 39

"EVERY MAN AND his dog is here," said Dusty, as we entered the Courthouse Markets the following Sunday morning. People swarmed along the aisles and milled around various tented stalls. Above the drone of voices around us came the sound of a live band thumping out a Beatles song with a didgeridoo accompaniment. The smell of sizzling kebab meat mingled with the pungent aroma of Thai spices and the sweet smell of donuts.

Dusty and I were escorting Jack to the masseur who operated under the boab tree. Using an online map to guide us, we weaved our way through the throngs of people, past various stalls displaying silk scarves, artworks, pearls, leather goods, soaps and candles to eventually arrive at the boab tree. Pink massage mats were lined up on the ground.

"Pink!" said Jack with a grin. "To match my hair." She had earlier had her spiked white peaks dyed pink. Dusty had diagnosed this as a reaction to her loss of Spratt and recommended Jack also pamper herself with a massage. Leaving Jack to her 'blissful fate', we set out to explore the markets.

The weather was already warm enough to stir a desire in me for a cold drink. We paused at a stall offering homemade lemonade and a shady canopy where customers could drink the refreshing beverage. After finishing her lemonade, Dusty placed her glass on the counter with an appreciative smile at the attendant then checked her phone.

"A message from Matilda," she said, moving clear of the counter to allow others to place their orders. "The authorities in Kenya managed to get in touch with Oliver Mayer's chess partner. He backs up Oliver's story and, in fact, still has an electronic record of their game with the time and date. We're running out of suspects."

Muriel Brown had been taken off the suspect list during the week when Inspector Lyons had contacted Dusty with the astonishing news that the confession Noelene's friend had made was false.

I was perplexed. "Why would she do something so stupid?"

"The psychiatrist who assessed her thinks Muriel felt so guilty about stalking Fern, she believed she needed to be punished."

"Jaysis!" I couldn't help myself. Surely even Muriel had more sense than that?

Dusty's reaction was compassionate. "Poor Muriel. When Inspector Lyons asked her whether she'd followed Fern, she admitted to the stalking and went on to say she'd killed Fern, Petra and Vicki. Her confession didn't ring true so Matilda asked for a second psychiatric assessment. Muriel's been released and sent home after a stern warning about wasting police time." This information had put paid to Noelene's concerns about police coercion.

"Does this take us back to Blake Montgomery?" I took another gulp of my cold lemonade.

"I think you've hit the nail on the head. We have to go back to one of the suspects we've eliminated…" Dusty paused. "Unless…"

I waited.

When she finally continued, she spoke haltingly as if she were still formulating her ideas. "Unless the killer is someone we haven't considered. Someone who seems an improbable murderer."

"For example?"

"Tavish."

"Tavish?" Her name was unusual enough for me to remember the cook at Pearl's Shell. Why Dusty would consider her a suspect had me flummoxed. Until I saw the grin spreading across her face.

"Sorry. Couldn't resist a little joke."

I relaxed and joined in on the gag. "If Tavish was going to kill anyone it would be a man."

Dusty laughed. "All right. Let's get serious. Let's consider Noelene Hyett."

"I thought you said you were being serious."

"I am." Seeing the disbelief on my face, Dusty put her hand up to ward off my objections. "I did say improbable."

"Right. What's her motive?"

"That's the problem. No motive."

"And no opportunity, at least not for Fern's murder. She was watching horror movies with Muriel that evening." I stretched across to the counter to return my empty glass as we continued on our walk.

"I know. I just thought I'd say it out loud to make sure I felt comfortable eliminating her. Only by eliminating the impossible can we get to the truth."

"However improbable?"

"Exactly!" Dusty grinned, pleased I had picked up on her subtle reference to Sherlock Holmes. "So let me try out another suggestion on your sceptical mind." She paused for dramatic effect.

"What if Muriel's false confession was a clever double bluff?"

I was tempted to point out a 'clever double bluff' might not come easily to Muriel. Dusty distracted me with an excited cry. She'd been scrolling on her phone as we walked along.

"It *is* her!" She held the phone out to show me what she was looking at. "An old photo on Facebook. Look!" Muriel, Rhona and Noelene stood together at Pearl's Shell smiling for the camera. "She's wearing the belt, the murder weapon."

Before I could inspect the image, Dusty swiped her phone to take a text message. One hand clamped over her open mouth as she read it.

"It's from Muriel. She's at Gantheaume Point." She angled the phone to show me the text which read: *Am at the Point. Want to tell you everything before I go. Police would not believe me.*

I barely had time to finish reading before Dusty started running, calling over her shoulder. "She's going to jump."

# CHAPTER 40

WHEN WE ARRIVED at Gantheaume Point, we saw a curious group of tourists who had ceased their activities to stare up at Muriel standing on top of a deep red boulder jutting out over the ocean like a plank laid out over the side of a ship. She stood on the edge peering down.

Dusty and I scrambled up the red rocks as fast as we could.

Muriel turned at the sound of our approach and called out. "Only Dusty Kent. No one else comes up or I jump."

I didn't want to let Dusty continue on her own, but what choice did I have? When she reached the rock and started to climb onto it, Muriel insisted Dusty remain at the base. I couldn't help feeling relieved about that. Dusty was already in a precarious position. Her slight frame would be no match for any gust of wind. If she was on the boulder with Muriel, she could slip or be blown over the edge in an instant.

Dusty tried to coax the suicidal woman to safety. "Come away from the edge, Muriel. You're making me feel scared. You said you wanted to tell me something. Come here and talk to me."

"It's all right." A knowing smirk lingered on Muriel's face. "I'm going to be a mermaid. Mermaids are beautiful."

Worried for Dusty's safety, I took a few tentative steps closer while they were speaking.

"The police didn't believe me. But it was all true. I want someone to know the truth so no-one else gets the blame. I want you to tell my story."

"The police didn't believe you because you didn't seem to know the details of the murders."

"I forget things, that's why. When I get stressed I forget things. Now I've written it down and signed it and dated it. That makes it official, doesn't it? It's in there." She pointed to a small canvas bag at her feet. "I wrote down everything I did; even how I put frangipanis in their hair after I killed them. I like frangipanis." A frisson of fear chilled my body. Only the murderer could have known about the frangipanis. Muriel bowed her head and mumbled. "It was a game. It didn't feel like it was real."

Distant sirens announced the impending arrival of police and ambulances.

Muriel kicked the bag toward Dusty who retrieved it and took out a notebook. I could see the writing on the cover. *Muriel's Confession.* Dusty opened the book. As she scanned what was written there, she alternated between looking at the page and keeping an eye on Muriel who stood with her back to the ocean watching Dusty.

I took the opportunity to creep a little closer. In the split second when both Dusty and I had our eyes off Muriel, she turned and jumped, calling goodbye as she went over the edge.

I reached Dusty at the precise moment she realised what had happened. She screamed. "Muriel!"

In her agitation she lost her balance and teetered over the edge. I grabbed her arm. She dangled above the ocean for a split second before I managed to pull her back to safety, surprised at my own strength. Dusty fell against me, her heart pounding.

During this I had been dimly aware of someone else clambering up the rocks. "No!" Dusty jerked her head around at the sound of Noelene's voice. "Brownie!"

Noelene clambered up onto the boulder where Muriel had been, raced to the edge and looked down at the sea swirling around the jagged rocks below. She was perilously close to the edge. I moved Dusty to a safe position and made to climb onto the boulder. To my surprise, Dusty stopped me with a sudden grip of my arm. She was glaring at Noelene's back. I have seen Dusty angry and I have seen her upset but I have never seen her like this. Her face was contorted with rage. Nostrils flaring. Fists clenched. Eyes narrowed.

Noelene turned, shoulders slumping. It was too late to save her friend.

"It was you!" Dusty shouted at her. "You made Muriel do this."

Noelene stared at her in disbelief. "Me?"

"You killed those women. It was your belt." Dusty swiped her phone and held it up. "That's you on Facebook wearing the belt used to kill Vicki and Petra."

Noelene looked at the photo. "That belt? I gave it to Brownie ages ago."

It seemed like a plausible explanation. I expected Dusty to back off. However, she had only got started. "You gave yourself away. You knew what time Fern was murdered. Precise details about time of death had not been released to the public."

Police helicopters whirred in the background. Noelene clambered down off the boulder keeping her distance from Dusty.

"What are you talking about?"

"When I came to see you at your home, you gave Muriel an alibi for the night Fern was killed. You said you and Muriel were together at ten-forty-five." Dusty had not spoken about this to me. Now that she mentioned it, I recalled Noelene making the comment.

Noelene lost patience with Dusty. "For heaven's sake! It must have been a slip of the tongue. I would have meant seven-forty-five. That's when Muriel arrived at my place." Her eyes rested briefly on Muriel's notebook which had fallen from Dusty's grasp earlier. "I've had enough of this." She began to make her way back down the rocks.

Dusty bent and picked up the notebook. In it Muriel had scrawled a full confession. The last line was poignant. *They were beautiful and popular. They had everything I never had. That's why I did it.*

"This is rubbish! Noelene did it, Sean."

I wondered why Dusty was so sure Noelene was the killer. Why would Noelene want to murder her friend Petra and the other two women? It didn't make any sense. Why was Dusty so determined to ignore Muriel's last words? I kept my mouth shut for the time being; Dusty needed to calm down.

We stayed at Gantheaume Point while the coast guard recovered

Muriel Brown's body. Dusty texted Jack to explain why we had left her behind at the markets. A uniformed police officer took our statements and we gave Muriel's written confession to Inspector Lyons who had arrived with the police contingent. She had received a frantic message from Noelene who said Muriel had called to tell her what she planned to do. Dusty said nothing about her belief that Noelene was responsible for the murders but told the Inspector she would call in to the station to speak with her soon.

# CHAPTER 41

THE DAY OF Muriel's funeral service was a warm twenty-eight degrees Celsius, although I overheard one of the locals complain it was 'a bit nippy'.

Dusty, Jack and I had spent the previous evening witnessing the spectacular natural phenomenon known as Staircase to the Moon. This event coincided with a special anniversary for Dusty: the date of her mother's disappearance in 1988. While we waited for the moon to perform, Dusty told me she had finally received the results of the DNA tests carried out on tissue samples taken from human remains believed to be that of her mother. The burial site had been found in bushland near Dusty's hometown two years ago. Tests on those samples conducted in a laboratory in the United States confirmed the remains were those of her missing mother. The finality of this confirmation must have been a jolt for Dusty.

The bustling crowds of tourists around us became quiet as the full moon rose sedately, its deep orange radiating across the dark sky. A narrow strip of amber appeared as its reflection fell over the exposed tidal flats of Roebuck Bay, creating the illusion of a stairway leading straight up to the moon. A silent moment of peace and stillness descended before the crowd stirred; murmuring, gasping and clicking their cameras. For Dusty, the moment of stillness continued. She was oblivious to what was happening around her. Her face was glowing, her eyes shining when she came out of her trance. With Jack and me walking beside her, she began to skip, grinning up at us with a sort of childlike happiness.

Later, when she had returned from her otherworld, Dusty tried to explain her feelings. "It was like a part of me, or maybe a part of my spirit, floated up the staircase all the way to the moon. I can't put it in words. It has to do with my mother. All I know is, I now have an exquisite moment and a heavenly image to associate with Mum. It feels good."

Jack put it more plainly. "You let go of your burden of grief."

Now, standing at the gravesite of Muriel Brown in the Broome Cemetery, Dusty was more sombre.

Muriel's ex-husband, a bulky truck driver in his late fifties, had travelled to Broome to attend her funeral. He described the Muriel he knew as 'a bit shy but articulate, intelligent, creative and lots of fun'. He told Dusty he called into Broome from time to time to meet up with Muriel after their divorce and noticed how she changed. It baffled him.

"She'd always been captivated by fairies and fantasy, but it was just an interest." He ran a chunky hand across the bristles on the tip of his chin. "Recently though, it was almost as though she was living in a fantasy world. I even thought she might have been on dope, but Muriel always hated drugs."

"Drugs aren't the only things that change people's personalities and behaviour," said Jack as we moved away. "A person experiencing a traumatic event like divorce is vulnerable and can become easy prey for someone to manipulate. From what you've told me about Muriel, she seemed to have displayed all the signs of being a passive personality who has been made to feel worthless by a stronger, more dominant person. Similar to someone being regularly abused by a partner. The dominated person gradually loses all sense of self and becomes dependent. A woman can enter the relationship as a highly intelligent, socially adept, emotionally stable human being and become unrecognisable even to herself." Although referring to Muriel and Noelene's odd friendship, I realised Jack was probably also speaking from personal experience.

Dusty nodded, grim-faced. "Somewhere in my subconscious, I think I knew Noelene's friendship with Muriel had a hidden agenda." Her eyes rested briefly on Noelene a short distance away with a group of people. Any residual euphoria she might still be feeling from the previous evening dissipated.

"Poor Brownie," Noelene was saying. "I know she wrote a confession in her suicide note but I didn't want to believe it. I accepted it only when the police found the murder weapon in her flat."

Dusty's nostrils flared. I put a hand out to restrain her.

"She put the belt in Muriel's flat," said Dusty through clenched teeth as she turned away in disgust. "Right after Muriel jumped, she raced back home, got the belt and took it to Muriel's before the police or anyone else got there."

I had thought at the time how odd it was for Noelene to leave the scene before the emergency services had found Muriel's body. She might have been in shock; people in shock react in different ways. However, Dusty was not making any excuses for Noelene. Nor was she making excuses for herself; frustrated at her mistake in missing what she believed was Noelene's slip of the tongue.

"She gave herself away that morning we went to see her at her home and I didn't even notice. It wasn't until I saw the murder weapon around her waist that it came to me, came gushing up out of my subconscious."

"What did?"

"Sorry, Jack. I forgot you weren't with us at Noelene's home. Noelene said her neighbour could vouch for the fact she and Muriel were at her place watching a horror movie at ten-forty-five. How did she know what time frame to use for the alibi she gave Muriel? Which was actually an alibi for herself. Since she claimed to know nothing about Muriel killing the women, how did she know what time Fern was murdered?"

Even when the police found a golf club in the boot of Muriel's car, which forensic evidence later confirmed was the weapon used to stun Petra and Vicky, Dusty was not swayed from her conviction that Noelene Hyett was the killer. However, she had been unable to convince Inspector Lyons of Noelene's guilt. The Inspector pointed out that only the murderer could have known the details outlined by Muriel in her suicide note.

"Exactly," said Dusty. "The murderer gave her all those details.

Doesn't it strike you as strange that Muriel was not able to supply you with specifics during her first confession? That was because she didn't know much about the murders at the time. Since then Noelene told her everything."

"Why? It's hardly in the woman's interests to admit to murder, even to a friend."

"Unless she had manipulated Muriel into taking the blame and killing herself."

"If that's what you believe happened, bring me some evidence and a motive. Then I will bring Noelene Hyett in for questioning." Despite this offer, it was clear the Inspector did not believe Dusty would find anything against Noelene. To make matters worse, she went on to drop a bombshell. "You'll need to be quick, she's leaving for overseas in five days."

Dusty was taken aback. Noelene was not due to leave on her overseas trip for another two months. According to the Inspector, she'd brought her departure date forward because she finds Broome too depressing after what happened.

"Ms Hyett did the right thing by checking with us first," said Inspector Lyons. "She's not behaving like a criminal on the run."

"Noelene's leaving because she knows I'm onto her," Dusty said later. "You can bet your bottom dollar she won't return to Broome."

After her meeting with Lyons, Dusty set herself the task of scrutinising all of her notes and the police files and going over all the interviews she had conducted. I was charged with using my 'maze master' skills to check every detail of Noelene's life. Jack was given the job of finding out what she could by talking to locals.

"We have a new focus," said Dusty. "Concentrate on Noelene Hyett. We need to find out what we've missed."

Dusty also spoke with Noelene's work colleagues but was disappointed to draw a blank there. The only negative comment uttered was that Noelene was 'a bit stand offish'.

By the eve of Noelene's flight to Perth to catch her connecting flight to London it was beginning to look like Dusty was wrong about her. At breakfast that morning she expressed her frustration. "There must be something somewhere that will convince Inspector Lyons to arrest that cunning, conniving, murdering female viper." Dusty bit fiercely into a piece of toast scraped with Vegemite.

Jack was gazing at my Akubra which I'd flung into a corner chair. "You said Noelene used to go to the camel farm with Muriel. I know it's a long shot, but maybe someone out there knows something. I think I'll have a snoop around."

"Okay," said Dusty. "Check on Benji while you're there. He'll be missing Muriel." She grinned at me. "Better take Sean with you; he's good with camels."

I begged off with the excuse I had to continue my cyber research.

I don't think any of us believed Jack would find new information at the camel farm. We could not have foreseen she would return with a lightning bolt of evidence.

# CHAPTER 42

JACK'S EXCITEMENT, WHEN she came back over an hour later, was evident from the moment she slammed her car door and raced helter-skelter into the beach house, dancing around the living area, holding a notebook above her head. When she stopped dancing, she came to a halt in front of Dusty and me to give us a closer look. What she was displaying was a thick, obviously often-used notebook. Scrawled across the cover were the words, *Muriel's Journal*.

"It's a meticulous record of the murders," said Jack. "I found it at the bottom of Benji's feed bin where Muriel kept extra oats and wheat for him." She held the book out and fanned the pages. "You were right, Kent. They were in on it together. Noelene was the leader; Muriel was her willing accomplice."

"Eureka!" Dusty jumped up and hugged Jack.

"Every day in Muriel's life since they started planning the murders is recorded in this." Jack handed the notebook to Dusty.

Dusty immediately became engrossed in it, pausing occasionally to read relevant excerpts aloud.

"This is chilling stuff. Listen. *Last night Noley came up with a big idea and she's included me. I'm so excited. We're going to play a murder game; sort of like reality TV, but with a twist. It has to be planned carefully so we don't get caught.* She goes on to explain how they are going to carry out the perfect murder, outlining their step by step plans leading up to the killing of each victim." Dusty glanced up at me. "Your question about why the three victims used the alley instead of the new walkway is answered here. Noelene and Muriel prepared a sign directing people to use the old alley because the new walkway was out of order. Once the 'target' had entered the alley, Muriel whipped the sign off and hurried back to the car to wait for Noelene."

"Right." I was still reeling from the shock of discovering Muriel had written down the details of the murders, writing about them as some sort of thrilling game.

"All three murders were carried out the same way," continued Dusty. "Listen to what she wrote the day after Fern was killed. *What an amazing experience! Noley did it. She went up the alley and waited. But I had an important role. I was the target spotter. When I saw a target, I put our sign over the council sign. I was the getaway driver too.* They used Muriel's car. Parked it a short distance away from the marina. She describes how, after Fern's murder, they drove back to Noelene's place. Once again they parked the car a short distance away then crept into the unit from the back because they wanted Mrs Chi to think they'd been there all evening. They'd left the television on, the lights on, even the air conditioner. When they came back they made even more noise to attract the attention of their neighbour."

"Right. Why did they choose Fern Parkes?"

"They didn't. She was a random victim." Dusty glanced down at the journal. "This is what Muriel wrote the next day. *We took out a movie star! What a thrill. I hope it doesn't complicate things.*"

"It's sickening stuff to read," said Jack.

"I know. Everything is detailed here. How they chose the marina to commit the murders because of the absence of CCTV there. How they changed the number plates on Muriel's car. The actual killings are the only parts Muriel hasn't recounted in detail. I think that's because she didn't witness the murders."

"Which is why she couldn't give the details to the police when she first went to confess," I suggested. "Why did she make a false confession?"

"I think she panicked," said Dusty. "When the police wanted to question her about stalking Fern, she thought they were on to them and decided to take the blame. She wanted to protect Noelene. You know what? I don't think Noelene knew about this journal. It'll be interesting to see how she reacts."

# CHAPTER 43

NOELENE, DRESSED IN jeans and T-shirt, offered us a cool reception on her front step. Through the open doorway I could see several large suitcases, packed and labelled.

"What do you want? If you've come to accuse me of murder again, you can leave right now."

Dusty was equally cool but polite. "I apologise for disturbing you. We found something belonging to Muriel I'd like to ask you about."

"Poor Brownie. Can't you let her rest in peace?"

Dusty reached into her bag, withdrew Muriel's journal and held it up so Noelene could see the cover. "Muriel has very kindly left a detailed record of how you two planned and carried out the three murders."

Noelene's eyes were fixed on the journal, her posture rigid. She recovered herself almost immediately, twisting her mouth in a scornful sneer.

"Brownie lived in a fantasy world. I'm not saying she was a liar but she would write about the way she wanted things to be; not the way they actually were. If she says I helped her commit those dreadful murders, it's because she wished I was with her. I knew nothing about what she was doing. If I had, I'd have put her straight."

"It's odd she didn't mention it. I had the impression she shared most things with you. She describes the murders as the biggest adventure of her life and yet she told you nothing."

"She knew I'd be horrified." Noelene gripped the door jamb and stepped back ready to close the door. "That's probably why she wrote about it, because she didn't have anyone to tell. I'm very sorry about the deaths of Petra and the other two ladies. But Brownie is dead; she paid for what she did. I suggest you leave it at that."

Dismissing Dusty as though she were a recalcitrant child was not a wise move. If her determination to nail Noelene was already at the highest possible level, I was sure it just went through the roof. She turned before Noelene had a chance to shut the door and marched, grim-faced, back to the car.

We drove straight to the police station to hand Muriel's journal over to Inspector Lyons.

"Noelene Hyett is correct," said the Inspector after scanning through the notebook. "These notes do look like delusional ramblings. Muriel Brown doesn't give any details of the actual killings here. It's almost as if she wants to distance herself from the act of murder, as though she doesn't want to admit to herself what she has done. Not until she is about to die does she have the clarity to do so; hence the detailed confession in her suicide note. There's nothing in here to suggest Noelene Hyett had a motive to kill any of the three victims."

"In the journal, Muriel says the actual target is Petra. That could be Noelene's motive. She was jealous of Petra. Might have even had a falling out with her." The Inspector raised a sceptical eyebrow. Dusty pressed her point. "Noelene's mind could be warped because of what happened to her as a teenager. She could harbour a deep jealousy of women who are happy and seem to have had a blessed life."

Inspector Lyons remained sceptical. "I can't bring murder charges against Ms Hyett based on this journal." The Inspector held her hand up to fend off a vigorous protest from Dusty. "However, I can bring her in for questioning."

Dusty came away from the police station determined to find something to convince the Inspector. By now, I was starting to have doubts myself. I recalled how distressed Noelene had been when she found out Muriel was under interrogation by the police. I pointed this out to Dusty.

"She seemed to me to be genuinely worried about her friend," I said.

"She was worried; worried about what Muriel might reveal. She thought her accomplice might give the game away." Dusty turned to me, her hands in the prayer gesture. "You're my last hope, Mr Maze Master. Noelene's plane leaves tomorrow. You've got to find some evidence she wanted to harm Petra."

All I had discovered about Noelene so far through social media and other websites was unremarkable. Her parents are divorced; her mother works in a remote community in the Kimberley, her father lives in Perth. She studied for her early childhood education diploma at the local TAFE Institute, has worked at Forrest Road Early Learning Centre for eight years. Prior to that she worked at another childcare centre two hundred kilometres away. Career opportunities drew all of her siblings to other parts of Australia and overseas where they had each established highly successful careers in areas like film and television and marketing. I went to the library to read a local newspaper article about the kidnapping and attempted rape of Noelene. It was a short piece revealing nothing more than what we already knew.

Inspector Lyons questioned Noelene but released her without charge. Noelene was apparently calm and co-operative during the interview. She also agreed to a police search of her home. Nothing was found connecting her to the murders.

The next day we still hadn't discovered anything that could be used as evidence. Jack, who had been keeping Dusty's prime suspect under surveillance, reported Noelene had caught her flight to Perth.

"She's going to get away with it!" Dusty paced up and down the living area, running her hands through her hair. She was mindful we had only a few hours before Noelene would board her flight to London. Once there, Dusty was convinced she would go underground. "We've got to do something." She stopped pacing to stare out the window.

Disappointed my maze-master skills had failed to be effective in this instance, I offered a forlorn excuse. "I don't know where else to look. There's not much about Noelene on the internet, not even a whisper about her Lotto win. She must have done a good job of keeping it quiet."

Dusty stopped pacing and turned to stare at me. "Sean O'Kelly!

You're a genius!"

"Is that a level above maze master?"

"Don't joke. This is serious. I think you've cracked the case. These murders were about money."

# CHAPTER 44

THINGS MOVED FAST after that. Dusty and I went to speak with Greg Birch who was back in Broome. Jack went to Forrest Road Early Learning Centre and retrieved the contents of Petra's pigeon hole. I put my maze-master skills to very effective use. Eventually we had enough evidence to convince Inspector Lyons Noelene Hyett had motive for murder. Noelene was detained at Perth Airport as she was about to board her London flight and was now being brought back to Broome. Dusty called Inspector Lyons and the people she had interviewed, inviting them to a meeting the following day for an update on her investigation into the murder of Fern Parkes. Curiosity about what had happened to Fern was not the only incentive to attend. An invitation to a private gathering by a famous author is not an event that happens every day in a small town like Broome.

We all gathered at Diamond Box Cocktail Bar at eleven o'clock. Despite the warmth of the morning, Dusty was wearing a light cardigan over her sleeveless ochre-red dress. She had bought a pair of pearl teardrop earrings at the Courthouse Markets and was wearing those today. I could see glimpses of turquoise in her multicoloured thong-sandals.

Dusty had reserved the whole outdoor area to ensure some level of privacy for the meeting. The tables had been pushed to the back. At the front, several chairs were arranged in a semicircle within reach of a long narrow table laden with small plates of finger food, jugs of water and glasses. An elegant silver ice bucket surrounded by long-stemmed champagne glasses served as the centrepiece. Nestled in the ice were several bottles of champagne. Dusty stood a short distance in front of this table, facing the audience. I sat with my laptop at a small table diagonally behind her.

Inspector Lyons, looking impressively official in full uniform, sat next to Shama and Rhona at one end of the semi circle. Oliver Mayer and Greg Birch sat in the middle with an empty chair between them. Several chairs separated the two men from Blake who sat at the opposite end, a glass of scotch in front of him on the table. Wasim had pulled a chair forward from the back and sat behind the others. When he saw Jack also taking a chair from the back, he hurried to carry it for her. She accepted his gallantry with a smile and directed him to place her chair next to his. Kayla was not there as she had not returned Dusty's calls. Noelene Hyett would be brought to the meeting by the police officer escorting her when they arrived in Broome.

Dusty began by announcing Muriel Brown was not the killer of the three young women whose bodies had been found at Queen City Marina several months ago.

"The murderer almost got away scot free. It was as a result of an insightful remark from my assistant here," Dusty gestured towards me, "that I finally hit on the motive. This was confirmed when I went to see Petra's friend, Greg Birch." She inclined her head in Birch's direction.

He was one of those ruggedly handsome Australian men who exude outdoors and make Irish computer geeks feel deficient. His dark hair, brown eyes and swarthy skin gave him an aura of mystery women might find hard to resist.

I had accompanied Dusty when she visited him at his photographic studio in Broome. The walls were lined with stunning examples of his work: a kangaroo racing across a pristine beach, a yellow monitor lizard standing on its hind legs peering at the landscape like a reptilian meerkat, and a magnificent shot of a humpback whale rising out of the ocean in a fusillade of water.

Dusty asked Birch about Petra's friendship with Noelene.

"They were good mates."

"I understand they were hoping to go overseas together. Did you know about that?"

"Yeah. Petra and I kept in touch after we broke up. I mean, the occasional email and she'd pop in here from time to time to look at my latest photos."

"So it was an amicable split?"

Birch looked at her quizzically. "You sound surprised."

"I heard a rumour about you being too controlling."

"Controlling? Hardly. I admit I became too possessive. I didn't realise I was but when I looked back on our relationship afterward, I could see it. It was after we split that Petra and Noelene decided on the overseas trip."

"Did you know they each took out separate Lotto tickets hoping to win money for the trip?"

Greg Birch grinned. "Petra didn't take it too seriously. She knew the chances of having a big win, or even a medium win, on Lotto were almost nil. She wasn't one of those people who watched the draw and checked their numbers straight away. Her ticket stayed in her pigeon hole at the child care centre until the next one was due."

"How do you mean?"

"The girls had a monthly ticket. When the month was up, Petra would check the results online then give Noelene the money to play it again for the next four weeks."

"So Noelene was the one who went to the Lotto agency and put the tickets on?"

"Yeah. I'm pretty sure that's the way they did it. Noelene used to go down to the street to run errands for the childcare centre. While she was out she'd do the Lotto tickets. When she came back she'd slip Petra's into her pigeon hole. It stayed there until it was time to play it again."

"Do you happen to know what Petra's numbers were?"

Greg shook his head. "She always used 26 which was her birth date and 9 which was the date she arrived in Australia from South Africa. I don't know what her other numbers were. I know she only ever played one game a week and Noelene did the same on her ticket, I think."

After our meeting with Greg Birch, I had utilised my maze master skills to access Petra's online Lotto account as well as Noelene's. However, it would not be wise to reveal to someone like Inspector Lyons too many details of how I did it. Dusty managed to cleverly step around that issue now as she outlined details of the case to her audience.

"My team was able to establish that the last monthly Lotto ticket Petra Venter bought started on January 7. The first prize for the draw on the seventh of January was thirty million dollars. The winning ticket was Petra's." Those seated in front of Dusty reacted with a collective gasp of astonishment. "But Petra didn't check her ticket. It was her habit to wait until all four games had been played before doing so. In this case, the last game would have been played on January 28. By that time, Petra was dead. She died on January 21."

Greg Birch buried his head in his hands.

Dusty explained the pigeon-hole system used by Petra and Noelene.

"It was clear to me that Noelene, when she realised Petra's ticket had won first prize, substituted her own for the ticket in the pigeon hole. She now had a ticket worth 30 million dollars. At long last, she had the means to get out of Broome, to have complete freedom and to live a glamorous lifestyle, to show her successful siblings she was as good as they were. I believe jealousy was also a factor. She couldn't bear the thought of Petra being so wealthy while she remained a poorly paid childcare worker. An irresistible opportunity had presented itself. As the thought of having so much money grew in her consciousness, the idea of not having it became unbearable. She developed a desperate desire to do whatever she had to in order to make sure the money became hers. She knew she would have to get rid of Petra before she checked her ticket online at the end of January." Rhona and Shama exchanged shocked glances. Dusty continued. "Although Petra didn't keep track of the numbers she used for Lotto, she would see immediately that the two numbers she knew well, 26 and 9, weren't on the ticket she was checking. It wouldn't take her long to work out Noelene had swapped the tickets over."

Rhona's face blanched at the realisation her volunteer at Pearl's

Shell was a ruthless killer. She might also have been contemplating the irony of her apprehension about Muriel when in fact Noelene was the one who should have made the hairs on the back of her neck stand up.

"Noelene Hyett came up with an audacious plan," said Dusty. "She would kill Petra. Not only would she murder her friend, she would kill two other women to make it look like a serial killer had done it. She realised it would be better not to kill Petra first. Her first target was a random choice but turned out to be a high profile celebrity, Fern Parkes."

A vein pulsed in Blake Montgomery's neck. He sprang from his seat and began to pace up and down. Dusty paused. She had warned everyone much of what she had to say today could cause them distress and gave them the option not to attend or to leave if they found it too painful. She might have been about to remind Montgomery he could choose to leave. However, he stopped pacing, raised a hand in apology and sat down again.

"Noelene's second victim was not chosen at random. This time she was after a specific target: her friend Petra Venter." Greg Birch shook his head in disbelief. "Her third victim, Vicky French, was chosen at random." Oliver Mayer listened with his head bowed.

"With Petra dead, no-one could challenge Noelene's claim to the winning ticket. There was nothing to prove it wasn't hers. Proof was what I needed. Proof Noelene had swapped the tickets over. The identity of the holder of the winning ticket was withheld by the Lotto agency, but my assistant established it was Noelene Hyett who cashed it in and claimed the 30 million. I knew Noelene would allege the winning ticket was her own regular ticket. I needed to prove it was rightfully Petra's. Unluckily for Noelene, I have another clever assistant." Dusty grinned over the heads of the audience at Jack.

With uncanny timing, that was the moment Noelene Hyett arrived. Everyone turned to study the woman they now believed to be a cold-blooded murderer. I was staring for another reason; I recognised the detective escorting her.

# CHAPTER 45

THE TWO UNIFORMED officers who were part of the escort remained at the entrance to the outdoor area. Although I recognised the bushy eyebrows of one of them from the day Dusty intervened in the domestic violence incident, my attention was held by the plain clothes detective who ushered Noelene forward. Detective Superintendent Thorn! I was intrigued to observe the only greeting exchanged between him and Inspector Lyons was a brief nod of acknowledgement.

Dusty gestured for Superintendent Thorn to bring his prisoner to the front. Heads turned to follow the pair's progress until they came to a halt near me. Dusty continued talking, keeping her eyes on Noelene.

"My assistant Jack went to Forrest Road Early Learning Centre on the off chance they had kept the contents of Petra's pigeonhole. They had. It wasn't until after Petra's family had returned to South Africa that the staff at the Centre remembered to clear it. The family declined their offer to post the contents to them as it contained nothing personal; just paperwork. The paperwork included Petra's Lotto ticket. At least, what should have been her Lotto ticket. However, the numbers on the ticket in Petra's pigeonhole match with the numbers Noelene Hyett regularly played. Now I had the evidence I needed."

A grim-faced Noelene returned Dusty's stare. Dusty spoke directly to her. "I think you left the ticket in Petra's pigeonhole to avoid raising suspicion among the staff who were aware of Petra's habit of leaving her Lotto ticket there. In fact, some of them joked with her, telling her they'd take it and claim it as their own if her numbers ever came up. Maybe that's what gave you the idea."

Noelene curled her lip in an indignant snarl. "I had nothing to do with Petra's death. I didn't murder anybody. I had no grand Lotto plot. Poor Brownie was jealous. That's why she killed the women, as she said in her confession."

"I'm disappointed you're still denying your guilt, Noelene. I hoped you would apologise to these people who cared about the women whose lives you ruthlessly cut short."

"I sympathise with those who are grieving." Noelene looked briefly at the people seated in front of her. "But I have no intention of apologising for something I didn't do."

"I include Muriel in the list of women you killed. I don't think you meant for her to die in the beginning. I believe the idea came to you after she went to the police station and made her first false confession. Muriel tried to take the blame for the murders in order to protect you. You took it one step further and, knowing how suggestible Muriel was, manipulated her into writing out a full confession and taking her own life. I think you played on Muriel's belief in fantasy to convince her she would become a mermaid after diving into the sea."

Jack glared at Noelene. "*You're* the only Satanist in Broome."

Dusty shifted her attention to Detective Superintendent Thorn.

"Have you had a chance to assess the likelihood of a conviction in this case based on the evidence we have?"

"As a matter of fact, I discovered more evidence."

"Serious?"

Thorn's eyes rested on Noelene. "Ms Hyett might have been clever enough to wear gloves during the murder and she no doubt thought she was being clever by leaving a frangipani to make police think the murderer was a male serial killer. However, her DNA was left on the frangipani flowers when she snipped them off the trees."

Noelene's face turned ashen, a clear indication she had, despite her careful planning, overlooked this small detail. Her reaction didn't go unnoticed by Dusty whose eyes gleamed with triumph.

"Excellent," she said to Thorn. "It removes any doubt about Muriel's guilt. Her DNA won't be on the frangipanis, only Noelene's."

"Correct."

Superintendent Thorn gestured to the Broome police officers who came forward to take an emotionless Noelene away. Dusty looked after them pensively before turning to Thorn.

"Can human DNA samples be extracted from plants?"

Thorn grinned. "I have no idea."

Dusty laughed. She has been known to bluff a suspect in the same way. Perhaps this tactic might have contributed to Thorn's reputation as a skilled interrogator famous for extracting confessions.

When Inspector Lyons made to follow the police officers escorting Noelene, Dusty stopped her.

"Matilda, please stay for a few moments. You must join us in a celebratory drink. You too, Superintendent Thorn."

I assumed the not unfamiliar role of barman to pour the champagne. Jack came forward to hand the drinks around. It wasn't until later that I learned Dusty had an ulterior motive for proposing the toasts. When everyone had a glass of bubbling champagne, she began with a toast to Fern, Petra and Vicki.

"To the lives they lived; to the people they were." We raised our glasses. "And a toast to celebrate the apprehension of their murderer." Dusty raised her glass with a triumphant flourish. "I am aware how much it means for family and friends to know what happened and why." We all joined her in the salutation.

With the toasting over, Dusty allowed Greg, Oliver and Wasim, each of whom assured her they would not be getting behind the wheel of a vehicle, to slip away. She asked the remainder of her guests to resume their seats. Superintendent Thorn chose Wasim's vacant chair behind the semi-circle where he sat with his legs stretched forward, crossed at the ankles.

Dusty's next statement was probably not what they were expecting. "Since this investigation really started with the death of Tiri Welsh in 2000, it seems appropriate I wrap up with Tiri."

# CHAPTER 46

DUSTY REACHED FOR a glass of water before she continued. "My investigation began because of Rhona's desire to bring her sister's killer to justice. She believed there could be a connection between these recent murders and Tiri's tragic death. Even though my team and I have been kept busy with the current investigation, I have given some thought to what happened the night Tiri died. Rhona has always believed Tiri was murdered, murdered by her husband Blake Montgomery."

"I still do." Across the empty chairs between them, Rhona's eyes were fixed on Blake.

"I came into this case with preconceived ideas about the guilt of Blake Montgomery based on what I'd read in the media. This perception was confirmed when I spoke to Rhona. As I got to know Blake, I started to question my assumptions." Rhona switched her stare to Dusty, eyebrows arched. Dusty ignored her. "I found him to be charming and sincere. I concluded he'd loved Tiri. However, I know abusive husbands often present a charismatic facade to the outside world. As I learned more about Blake I discovered he appeared to have been loyal to his wife. He resisted the advances of her younger sister and apparently refrained from becoming involved with his beautiful co-stars. In fact, Blake Montgomery was known in Hollywood as a devoted husband who did not play around. It might mean he was a man of principle who deserved my respect." Rhona snorted at this. "Or it could mean he had a dangerous obsession with Tiri."

Dusty locked eyes with Blake. "I'd like you to go over some of the details of the night Tiri died. The argument between the two of you started, you said, because Tiri got into a jealous rage when you mentioned another woman."

Rhona protested. "*He* was the one who got into jealous rages."

Blake looked across at Rhona. "You're right. I was prone to jealous outbursts. But I never raised a hand to Tiri or any other woman. That's the way I was brought up. It was ingrained in me. My father could see I had a tendency to lose control in fits of temper. He wanted to make sure he got that message through. Take your anger out on things if you have to, but never on people, he said, and never ever on a woman. If you get angry with a woman, walk away. If a woman gets angry with you, walk away. That's what he said. Most of the time when Tiri and I had a blazing row, I did walk away. On some occasions I would pick up something and smash it—"

Rhona interrupted him. "If you'd listened to your father, my sister would be alive today."

"Blake," said Dusty firmly, "the time has come to tell the truth about what happened to Tiri the night she died."

Rhona flung her accusation at Blake before he had a chance to respond. "You attacked her that night, didn't you? You pushed her overboard." Her eyes glistened.

Blake put his head in his hands. "I'm sorry, Rhona. I'm so sorry."

"It's too late for sorry." With her body tense, her fists clenched and her lips in a thin tight line, Rhona's anger was raw and visible; her desire to strike at Blake unmistakable. Shama restrained her with a gentle hand on her friend's arm.

"It was an accident." Blake's apparent attempt to excuse his actions caused Rhona to draw up her head in disdain. Blake held up his hand to appease her. "But it was my fault." His voice was barely audible. "I should have told the truth from the start."

Dusty prompted him. "You and Tiri were sitting out on the deck that evening, enjoying the warm night air. It was a perfect evening."

"Yes. It was like I told you, like I told the police. Tiri and I had finished our meal and were enjoying each other's company." He seemed reluctant to continue as if he didn't want to move away from the memory of being with Tiri on the deck.

"Then something went wrong. Tiri was angry because you suggested inviting one of your beautiful co-stars to spend time on the yacht with you both." Dusty turned to Rhona. "My amazing research assistant managed to confirm Tiri was known to be jealous of Blake's leading ladies. You must have been aware of that."

Rhona tossed her head and thrust her chin forward. "She had good reason to be jealous."

Blake shook his head but did not respond to Rhona's implied accusation. He reached out toward his glass of scotch. Almost immediately, he withdrew his hand, letting it fall to his side.

"Tiri and I argued on the deck and again in the cabin later. Things got very heated. She marched out of the cabin." He inhaled and released a long breath. Up to this point, his version of events was the same as that which he'd told the police at the time. I sensed he was about to reveal new facts. The silence in the room suggested everyone else had the same feeling.

"At one point, Tiri raced outside and went onto the swim step. It was right near our cabin. When I caught up with her, she had closed the gate and was standing on the edge of the step as though ready to dive in. She was crying. I begged her to come back onto the yacht but she yelled at me saying I didn't love her anymore and she might as well disappear in the ocean. I didn't believe she would dive into the water but I was afraid she might fall in. She was in an emotional state with a few glasses of wine under her belt. I stayed on the other side of the gate, trying to calm her. I thought if I opened the swim step gate and tried to get close to her, she might fall into the water." Tears welled in Blake's eyes.

As I watched him during this exchange, I understood I was seeing Blake Montgomery, the person, for the first time. Before today I had seen only Blake Montgomery acting a part. It dawned on me that he used his acting skills, perhaps subconsciously, as a defence mechanism, by intuitively slipping into an appropriate role when interacting with others.

"Did you strike her?" Dusty leaned forward. She focused intense concentration on Blake, a sure sign she had activated the Dusty Kent

Lie Detector.

"Of course he did," snapped Rhona.

Blake answered through gritted teeth. "I did not."

Dusty seemed satisfied with Blake's response but she didn't exempt him from further interrogation. "Forensic evidence shows Tiri had suffered a blow to her head," she said. "How do you explain that?"

"I can't explain it except I know it didn't happen while we were together. I assume she bumped her head against a part of the yacht during the fall. Before she fell, she did put her hand up to her head but not because she'd been hit. It was as if she was feeling dizzy. She started to sway so I reached over and grabbed her arm to steady her, to pull her back toward the yacht. She was still so angry at me she tried to yank her arm free. I knew if I let go she'd fall so I held on to her and tried to open the gate at the same time. We were struggling together…" Blake cast a despairing glance at Rhona, as though seeking her forgiveness. "She slipped and fell into the water. God forgive me for not protecting her, for not saving her." He bowed his head.

The suspended quiet that followed was evidence all of us in the room believed we were witnessing a man suffering heart wrenching remorse. Even Rhona's anger seemed less bitter.

# CHAPTER 47

"WHAT DID YOU do when Tiri went into the water, Blake?" Dusty did not want to miss the opportunity to clarify every detail of what happened that night.

"I don't have a clear memory of it."

"Do you remember throwing the lifebuoy to her?"

"Yes. I think it was just after she fell. I threw it in because it's standard procedure when someone goes overboard. I didn't think she'd need it. Tiri was a good swimmer. I assumed the shock of the cold water would be enough to cancel the effects of alcohol. I was sure she would swim back to the yacht. I called out to her; thought if she had trouble seeing the yacht in the dark, the sound of my voice would guide her. I couldn't see Tiri in the water. It was so dark. I kept calling out and asking her where she was. She didn't answer."

"When Tiri fell, did she cry out?"

Blake nodded.

"She screamed in fear because you pushed her in." Rhona's anger was in full force again.

"It wasn't like that." Blake appeared resigned, as though he didn't expect to be believed. "It was a sort of mixture of surprise and apprehension, that type of scream."

"What did you do when you realised Tiri wasn't swimming back to the yacht?"

"I raced up to the cockpit and transmitted the SOS, put as many lights on as I could, grabbed a torch and ran back down to the swim step and took my jacket off ready to jump in. Then the police launch arrived."

"Matilda?" The Inspector jerked her head up abruptly as though

Dusty's voice had interrupted her thoughts. "How much time had elapsed between the time you heard the scream and when you received the SOS call over the radio?"

"Six minutes."

"How can you be so precise?"

"We reacted at once to the scream and were already on our way before we got the SOS call. The time of the scream coincided with the change in the launch's status which is recorded in the instrument panel."

Dusty swung back to Blake. "Why was there a delay before you made the SOS call? This fact has often been commented on since Tiri's death. Some people see this as evidence you intended to kill her. They say you pushed her into the ocean and deliberately delayed calling for help to make sure she drowned."

Rhona put her head in her hands. Shama gave her shoulder a reassuring caress.

Anger flashed across Blake's face. "It's easy to say things; easy to make assumptions that suit your prejudices."

Dusty stood her ground. "It's not all assumptions, Blake. One private detective conducted a re-enactment on the *Tooting Moon* and estimated you should have been able to get up to the cockpit in two minutes at the outside. He allowed another minute for your being in a state of shock. The time between Tiri going overboard and you sending out the call for help should have taken no more than three minutes. Yet you took six minutes."

Blake locked eyes with Dusty. "I've never forgiven myself for that. But it was not deliberate. After the initial shock, I waited longer than I should have because…" He glanced at Rhona. "I expected Tiri to swim back to the yacht. I didn't know she'd bumped her head, didn't even consider it. I thought at first she might not be responding to my calls because she wanted to get back at me – make me suffer. It seems like such a stupid, stupid thing to think when I look back on it now. But at the time…" Blake shook his head. "If I'd acted quickly…"

Jack came forward to sit next to Blake.

Dusty turned to Inspector Lyons. "If her husband had acted

quickly, would Tiri Welsh be alive today?"

"That's a difficult question to answer."

Superintendent Thorn's attitude changed to one of alertness. He straightened in his seat and leaned forward, his interest heightened.

"You actually spotted Tiri's sarong in the water, didn't you, Matilda?" Dusty glanced down at the piece of paper in her hands. "These are the copies of your statement and Senior Sergeant Thorn's statement taken at the time of the tragedy. When you saw Tiri's sarong floating in the water, you called out to your colleague and got him to direct a light on the sarong. Senior Sergeant Thorn, or Spike as you called him at the time, was at the wheel and you were at the back of the boat. Is that right?"

"Yes. The colour of the sarong floating in the water caught my attention. As the launch got closer we heard someone on the yacht calling out. I later learned it was Blake Montgomery."

"What did he say?"

"Help! My wife fell overboard. Something like that."

"Could you see Blake clearly enough to observe what he was wearing?"

"We had no time to stop and think or look around."

"You didn't notice whether he had his jacket off ready to dive in?"

"We were responding to a mayday call; the adrenaline was pumping. I was thinking only of the rescue. A woman was in the ocean in danger of drowning. Every second counted. I dived in and swam straight to the sarong but Tiri Welsh wasn't there."

"You held up the sarong to let Spike know Tiri wasn't wearing it; it had simply been floating on the water. You called out to Spike, telling him you couldn't find Tiri. Is that right?"

"That is correct. She was nearby, but by the time I had located her and got her onto the launch, it was too late."

Dusty looked down at the notes. "Senior Sergeant Thorn mentions in his statement that when he first trained the light onto the sarong, he thought he saw Tiri's head. If her head was above water that means she was still alive."

"Oh, Tiri!" Rhona buried her face in her hands.

"Dear God," said Blake. "I never knew that."

"No, you didn't. Because Senior Sergeant Thorn later conceded it could have been his imagination or a trick of the light." Thorn shifted in his seat. His lips parted as though he was about to say something but he remained silent. "The thing is, when I read that, I started playing 'what if'. What if Tiri had been alive and struggling to stay afloat when the police launch arrived on the scene? It was possible. According to forensics the blow to her head had not rendered Tiri unconscious although she might have been dazed. She was an experienced swimmer and would have known what to do in order to stay afloat as long as possible. Was she alive when you found her, Matilda? Did she say anything?"

I wasn't sure what Dusty was fishing for. Did she think Tiri Welsh had said something to prove her husband had pushed her in? Surely Matilda would have reported such information at the time.

"No to both questions," said Matilda, shaking her head.

"Tiri *was* alive." Superintendent Thorn's voice was scarcely audible yet his words galvanized everyone in the room.

Matilda's body stiffened but she did not turn around to look at him.

# CHAPTER 48

Dusty eventually broke the silence. "Are you saying Tiri Welsh was alive, struggling to stay afloat, when Matilda reached her?"

Thorn cleared his throat. His answer was loud and firm. "I am."

Matilda shook her head.

With her eyes on Thorn, Dusty continued. "I also asked myself, what if Matilda was lying when she called out to Senior Sergeant Thorn that she couldn't find Tiri? What if she held the sarong up to show Thorn because she actually wanted to prevent him from seeing Tiri and from seeing what she was doing? It would have been a simple matter to hold Tiri's head under. By this time Tiri would have been dazed, disoriented and confused. With all the strength sapped out of her limbs, she would have been powerless to resist." Blake, Rhona and Shama stared at Dusty. I was as surprised as they were. "Is that what happened?" Dusty asked.

Thorn clenched his jaw. "I believe so."

"Matilda was in love with you, wasn't she?"

A pink tinge crept along Matilda's neck.

Superintendent Thorn chose not to answer Dusty's question. "As I said in my statement, we worked on Tiri giving her CPR. We couldn't revive her. When we stopped, I turned away to hide how upset I was. Matilda didn't know I could see her face reflected in the surface of a panel on the boat." He swallowed. "She was looking at Tiri and smiling; smirking really. It wasn't a clear reflection so, at the time, I thought I must have been mistaken."

"Something happened to change your mind," prompted Dusty.

Thorn hesitated, scratching the side of his head. Finally, he resolved to answer. "One evening Matilda and I were walking home from the pub after celebrating a big arrest. She…" he shrugged, paused then continued. "She came on to me, you know."

"You rejected her?"

"Yeah. Ever since the night Tiri died, I'd felt uneasy about Matilda. The picture of her smirking down at Tiri was always in the back of my mind. Even though I thought I'd been mistaken about what I'd seen, the image was always there. Besides, I wanted to keep our relationship on a purely professional basis. Things can get complicated otherwise."

"A sensible attitude." Dusty's eyes rested on me for the briefest of moments when she spoke those words. "So you made it clear to Matilda you weren't interested?"

"I did. She flew off the handle and accused me of still thinking of Tiri. In fact, she said I was even more besotted with Tiri now she was dead. Then she said: *I did it for nothing.*" Thorn was staring at Matilda's back.

"Did you ask her what she meant?"

"I did. She clammed up when she saw the look on my face and claimed she'd been talking rubbish under the influence of alcohol."

Rhona and Shama were staring at Matilda in disbelief. Matilda folded her arms across her chest and shook her head. Blake had retreated into his own world, although his glass of scotch remained untouched.

"Why didn't you report your suspicions, Superintendent Thorn?"

"I had nothing I could take to my superiors. Matilda was seen as a hero. She'd deny everything. It would be taken for sour grapes on my part because she was getting so much attention."

Dusty turned to Matilda. "I can see why you lost your heart to Spike." The faintest suspicion of a blush shaded Thorn's cheeks. "I can only imagine your heartbreak and frustration in trying to compete with Hollywood's most beautiful woman. A woman who recognised the power beauty and fame gave her and who used that power to control any man she wanted."

Matilda's reaction took everyone by surprise. A hint of triumph smeared her voice. "One night I had more power than she ever had; the power of life and death."

Dusty and Thorn exchanged glances. This was close to a confession.

I doubt Inspector Lyons, with her years of experience as a police officer, would have made such an admission had it not been for the combined effects of being thrown off balance by Thorn's revelations and the consumption of champagne. Dusty had given Jack instructions to keep Matilda's glass topped up with the aim of loosening her tongue.

# CHAPTER 49

"DO YOU REMEMBER one day when Jack was missing and we went in the car with Matilda to Kayla's office?"

Our small group was now standing around the table. Dusty was responding to my question about what had alerted her to Matilda's guilt. After her admission, Inspector Lyons had stood up, straightened her navy police jacket and walked out without saying a word.

"If you recall," continued Dusty. "She told us what happened that night, how when she got to the sarong Tiri wasn't there."

"Right. I recall. She said she hadn't seen Tiri at first."

Dusty thrust an approving finger at me. "I picked up that she was lying."

"The famous Dusty Kent Lie Detector?"

"Yep. I didn't get a chance to follow through at the time. I was distracted because of worrying about Jack. But it stayed with me." She turned to Superintendent Thorn. "What will happen to Matilda now?"

"I'm confident we have enough to charge her. I'll go and put things in motion right away." He shook hands with all of us, including Blake, and left.

"Hang on, Kent. How did you know Matilda had it in for Tiri Welsh? How did you know she was in love with the delectable Thorn?"

"Three words gave her away." Dusty looked at me. "You were there the day I asked her about Spike; the day we met her in Bedford Park. Did you notice how her voice softened when she said 'Spike and I'?" I had not. Dusty shook her head at my obtuseness and added, "It was a dead give-away."

An emotional Rhona hugged Dusty and thanked her profusely. To my surprise she approached Blake and offered him an embrace. After a slight hesitation, he accepted. No words passed between them but it was clear they had arrived at some sort of metaphorical meeting place.

When Blake took his leave of Dusty, he bemoaned the fact that his PA had returned to Perth.

"Did she say why?" When Dusty had extracted the truth from Kayla a few days ago, she had urged the PA to tell her boss. Kayla had obviously not heeded her advice because Blake shook his head.

"Apparently she needs to go to London to see her cousin."

Kayla's ears turned a deep pink almost matching the burgundy rims of her glasses when Dusty had confronted her. "Kayla Bassett is not your real name, is it?"

She might have sensed Dusty had unearthed the truth about her background. However, she wasn't going to capitulate without resistance. "What do you mean?"

"Kayla Bassett, full name Michaela Bassett, is in London running her independent book publishing firm. Since your CV is identical to hers, I have to conclude you are guilty of identity fraud."

"No! It's not like that. Michaela knows I'm using her name. It was her idea."

"Convince me." Dusty raised her eyebrows and waited.

Resigned to making a full confession, Kayla sighed. "Michaela's my cousin. We grew up together. We're like sisters. She was staying with me in Perth when Mr Montgomery's publisher advertised for a Personal Assistant to work with him in Broome." Kayla's cheeks flamed red. "I've always adored Blake Montgomery. To work closely with him would be a dream come true for me. So Michaela said she'd make it happen. I didn't take it seriously until she actually got the job."

"So when the time came for Michaela to fly up to Broome, you got on the plane instead of her?"

"Yes. Michaela went back to London. We didn't think there'd be much of a problem; the PA position is a short term contract while Mr

Montgomery is working on his autobiography. After that I'll go back to being me."

"You mean Zoe Austin?"

"Yes. I'm a real estate agent. I've never worked on a writing project before but Michaela helps me out via email. She did at first, anyway. After a while I sort of got the hang of it. I don't need her help much anymore."

"How do you get paid?"

"The money goes direct into a back account. Michaela set it up and gave me all the security information." Kayla gave Dusty a pleading look. "Do you have to tell Mr Montgomery?"

"You'd better tell him before I need to."

Kayla had apparently chosen to flee rather than own up to Blake.

"I'll have to continue on my own until the publisher sends a replacement." Blake's trademark charismatic grin illuminated his face. "Unless you can stick around and help me?" Dusty responded to the flirtatious twinkle in his eye with a laugh and a shake of her head.

Dusty, Jack and I did 'stick around' in Broome for a few days, not to help Blake with his writing, but for 'well earned R & R' as Dusty put it. One morning Rhona arrived at the beach house, looking radiant in a simple orange dress.

"I couldn't let you leave without thanking you all properly." She placed three impeccably wrapped packages on the table. "These are for you with thanks from the bottom of my heart. I hope they will remind you of Broome, as well as Tiri."

Breathless gasps from Dusty and Jack expressed their astonishment. Each package contained a lustrous strand of South Sea cultured pearls and matching earrings. Even my untrained eye could see their high quality.

"Dusty told me you have someone special in your life who might enjoy wearing beautiful pearls," Rhona explained when I opened my box. I was sure Ingrid would accept the gift as appropriate compensation for my extended absence.

Brushing aside our expressions of gratitude, Rhona accepted an offer of coffee.

Over coffee she told us Pearl's Shell was starting regular self-defence classes for women. "It's not an answer to domestic violence. It's about confidence. When a woman knows she has the power and the skills to take down an attacker, her confidence shines through. As a result, her risk of being attacked is reduced. When she is assaulted, she has a better chance of fending off her assailant, even if he is bigger and stronger."

"Self defence classes are an excellent idea, Rhona." Dusty gave her the thumbs-up.

"It was Roz who suggested it."

"Roz?"

"She's one of our clients. Has a brute of a husband. You might have seen her at Pearl's Shell; a young pregnant woman with a purple streak in her hair."

"Yep. I know who you mean." Dusty shot me a quick glance but said nothing about our encounter with Roz and Jimmy. "I could show the women a few moves myself if I didn't have to leave in a couple of days." Dusty had practised karate since childhood.

Rhona smiled her appreciation. "As it happens we found an excellent instructor. Wasim Smith from Tranquillity has volunteered his services once a week."

The conversation prompted my memory of the bikies Jack had set on Jimmy. Was the 'brute of a husband' even still alive? As soon as Rhona left I asked Jack.

"What did the bikies do to Jimmy?"

"Don't look so serious." Jack laughed. "He's not wearing concrete boots at the bottom of the ocean. Those guys aren't bikies; they're bikers."

"There's a difference?" Dusty looked nonplussed.

"Course there is, Kent. A bikie is a member of a gang. A biker is someone who rides a motorcycle."

Dusty pointed at me.

"Aye. Like Seamus." Jack grinned. "I mean, Sean. Anyway, my friendly bikers took Jimmy out and shouted him a few beers the night you stopped him from beating his wife in the street. They kept buying him drinks until he was so pissed he was incapable of carrying out any violence."

"Wouldn't he have belted into 'his woman' as soon as he sobered up?" I asked.

"Not in retaliation for what happened in the street. His type are knee-jerkers. He would have calmed down by the time he sobered up. But as soon as something else came up to provide him with an excuse, he'd beat her up again. All I did was buy her a short reprieve. You achieved more than that, Kent. Looks like your intervention prompted Roz to think about her situation."

"Good for her. Those self defence classes will help other women too." Dusty started rewrapping her gift from Rhona. "We'd better put these somewhere safe. They're worth stealing!"

"Which reminds me," said Jack. "Noelene won't be allowed to keep the 30 million dollars, will she?"

"She most certainly will not," said Dusty. "I've already checked that out. Her bank account has been frozen. When the legalities are finalised, the money will go to Petra's estate. In preparation for her overseas trip, Petra had made a will. She left everything to her parents in South Africa so the money will go to them."

"Good." Jack gave the thumbs-up before adding, "Seems odd no-one in Broome knew about her win. I know Lotto winners can have their names withheld but the newspapers usually publish where the winning ticket was sold."

"They do. But this was a special case. Because of the humungous prize money the lottery people, Lottowest, agreed to keep the location a secret for several months. Delaying the announcement would make it difficult for people to guess who the winner might be."

"Jolly decent of them," said Jack.

That evening, we were out on the open ocean heading for Rowley Shoals. Blake had invited us for an excursion on the *Doris* insisting we must experience the open ocean at night. He did not ask us to wear life-jackets this time. I wondered if that was because he had more confidence in our sailing ability. On the other hand, he could have developed anxiety about passengers without safety vests after what happened to Tiri. Now he was more relaxed, not only about that but also in a general sense.

Our cruise began with a glorious sunset over the water shortly after we left Broome. When we reached our destination, we stayed up late to enjoy the night time ocean experience. Out on the deck we gazed up at the moon and stars in the night sky. With softly spoken words, Blake began to recite an old poem, his eyes still on the moon.

"Lady Moon, Lady Moon, where are you roving?"

Dusty joined in. "Over the sea."

Blake acknowledged her contribution with a slight nod. "Lady Moon, Lady Moon, whom are you loving?"

Jack added the next line. "All that love me."

Blake seemed about to recite another line of Houghton's poem but hesitated and apparently changed his mind. "Tiri loved the moon." A nostalgic smile played across his lips. "As a child she dreamed of living on the moon." He turned to face us. Either the influence of the moon or the memory of Tiri had put a shine in his eyes and added radiance to his face. "That's why we called our yacht *Tooting Moon*. We wanted a name to symbolise our private world on the boat."

Gazing out at the dark ocean all around us, I realised being on the yacht, with its lights and comforts, gave those on board a sense of being in a capsule of intimacy.

"Why Tooting?" I asked.

"That's where I was born; Tooting in London. I had a blissful childhood there. The yacht was a sanctuary for us. We had our happiest times on *Tooting Moon*." Blake's expression became serious. "Until that last night." He shook his head. "Y'know, I thought I was moving on when I got rid of the yacht. The irony is, I reckon I've been trapped on *Tooting Moon* all this time."

Silence followed. Each of us was lost in our personal reflections. Blake was the first to speak.

"Y'know, I'll be roving over the sea again soon. It's time for me to leave Broome."

"Going to visit your daughter in the UK," suggested Jack.

Blake gave her an appraising look and nodded. "You got it,

Margriet. I need to spend some time with her. I might not go back to the States; maybe I'll stay in the UK."

"You could finish writing your autobiography there," said Dusty.

"I could. And I might. But I'm not sure I need to." He glanced up at the moon and recited another line of the poem. "Are you not tired with rolling, and never resting to sleep?"

The next evening we were back in Broome to spend our final night there. After leaving the Doris and saying goodbye to Blake, the three of us celebrated the closing of the case with pizza and drinks in the covered outdoor area of the beach house. It was a typical balmy Broome evening.

"By the way," said Dusty, tilting her glass of gin and tonic in my direction. "Thanks for saving my life." She turned to Jack. "I would have ended up the same as poor Muriel if Sean hadn't grabbed me the other day at Gantheaume Point. It was a real James Bond moment."

Jack bowed her head and tipped an imaginary hat to me. I concentrated on my Guinness.

Reluctance to face the reality of departure the next day might have been what kept us sitting there until almost midnight. When we did retire to our respective rooms, it wasn't for long. A strangled scream from the back of the house sent Dusty and I rushing to Jack's bedroom.

Jack was on the back porch gazing up into the tree canopy which was illuminated by soft light from Jack's room. Perched in his favourite spot, between the fork of two branches, was Spratt; his protruding brown eyes gazing down at us.

Jack turned her glowing face to us. "He came back to say goodbye. How good is that?"

As she spoke, Spratt used his hind legs to launch himself into the air, spreading his membranes on either side to become a tiny living parachute. He glided through the branches and disappeared from sight.

"He'll land on another tree, and go from tree to tree," said Jack. "Goodbye, dear Spratt."

"You're going to miss the cute little fellow." Dusty put her arms around her friend.

"I'll miss him to the moon and back." She stared up at the branch where Spratt had been. "But you know what they say. If you really love something you have to let it go."

"True," said Dusty. "You're an inspiration, Jack. Actually, you're a pearl."

"I am?"

"Yep." Dusty smiled. "Your name Margriet is the Dutch version of Margaret. Rhona told us Margaret comes from a Sanskrit word meaning pearl. So Margriet also means pearl."

"Fair dinkum? That must mean the world is my oyster. How about that!"

★

IT'S INTERESTING, ISN'T it, how a question can have the power to clarify an issue? When Dusty asked me just before we left Broome whether Ingrid and I had set a date for the wedding, I realised I have been avoiding making that commitment. Ingrid had suggested possible dates on a couple of occasions but we had not finalised anything because I kept coming up with excuses. Whenever I thought of walking down the aisle with my beautiful fiancé, Dusty's face appeared in my mind's eye. Now I'm wondering if I proposed to Ingrid out of some sort of subconscious desire to make Dusty jealous in the way Fern had taken a lover to stir Blake's feelings.

In my moment of reflection, I also recalled the look Dusty had given me when she agreed with Detective Superintendent Thorn that a romantic liaison would complicate a professional relationship. She was sending me a message. That single look also told me my anxiety about summoning up the courage to tell her how I felt about her had all been for nothing. She already knew. I believe she was also warning me not to put her on the spot, not to force her to reject me. The conversation I wanted to have with her would never eventuate.

Now I face a dilemma. Just as Blake Montgomery had been, I am trapped by my emotions. My grandmother would say I was lost in the woods. She also said: *If there's a way into the woods, there's a way out.* It's time to find my way out. It seems to me the answers to two questions will help me get my bearings. Am I certain I want to marry Ingrid? Should I resign from my job with Dusty?

★

# About the Author

Brigid George is the pseudonym of JB Rowley – author of *Whisper My Secret, Mother of Ten* (both Amazon #1 Best Sellers) and the children's series *Trapped in Gondwana*. Why Brigid George? Brigid because that was what JB's father called her. George because that was his first name.

JB Rowley grew up in a small Australian town called Orbost in the state of Victoria. She spent her childhood chasing snakes and lizards down hollow logs, playing Hansel and Gretel in the bush with her brothers, climbing trees, searching the local rubbish tip for books to read and generally behaving like a feral child. To avoid her boisterous brothers she often escaped into the hayshed with a book. Hours and hours of reading from an early age trained her for life as a writer. In primary school her teachers called her 'the one with the Enid Blyton touch'. Her love of reading murder mysteries as an adult has now evolved into a love of writing them.

As a teenager JB had short stories published in one of Australia's national magazines, *New Idea*. Since then she has won several awards for her stories which have also been published in anthologies.

Visit the website of Brigid George.
www.brigidgeorge.com

# Dedication

*The Dusty Kent series is dedicated to my father, George Rowley; a good man who died too young.*

# Further Information

The story of the missing box of diamonds in 1942 is true. Benji Bullet, the slow Australian racehorse, does exist and has never won a race.

The following are fictional:

Broome Satanists

Forrest Road Early Learning Centre

Ida Lloyd Museum (The wooden pearl lugger called Ida Lloyd did exist.)

Lottowest

Pearl's Shell

Queen City Marina

Sindbad, the cheeky camel (The camels used for the camel tours are more amenable than Sindbad.)

The Bamboo Garden

The Camel Farm

The giant chess set

The overhanging suicide rock at Gantheaume Point (There are rocks overlooking the ocean but the one in this book is fictitious.)

Tranquillity Wellness Centre

# Glossary

**Akubra hats:** (Akubra is pronounced 'UH – koo – bra') Iconic wide brimmed felt hats made in Australia.

**Bikie:** a member of a gang of motorcyclists

**In suspenders:** in suspense

**Piss someone off:** to make someone angry

**Pissed:** inebriated

**Vegemite:** a dark brown Australian food spread made from leftover brewers' yeast extract

**TAFE:** Technical and Further Education

## Review the book

If you have time to post comments after you read the book, that would be enormously helpful – just a few words is fine. Many thanks to all who have taken the time to review my other books. Don't forget to tell your friends about the Dusty Kent Mysteries.

## Mailing List

To get an automatic email when Brigid's next book is released, sign up here.

www.brigidgeorge.com/free-booklet.html

# Acknowledgements

My niece Sally introduced me to the place name Tooting for the first time during a trans-Atlantic phone call after she had relocated from Melbourne to London. Tooting seemed to me to be such an incongruous name for a London suburb that I asked Sally to repeat it several times. She did eventually convince me there was an actual place called Tooting. The name stayed with me and I resolved to one day use it in a book title.

Kay Wee, my unpaid Personal Assistant, named Blake Montgomery's PA.

My friend Margriet Benninga gave me permission to use her name for Jack.

For allowing me to use her name, I thank my good friend Tavish Fyfe with whom I shared many crazy moments when we worked together at 'the top pub' in Orbost.

Lisanne Radice, described by The Guardian newspaper as a UK 'publishing legend', has once again provided invaluable manuscript guidance.

BB eBooks has provided spectacular service and impeccable formatting for all of the Dusty Kent books and several of my other books.

Yocla Book Cover Designs designed the sensational cover.

Thank you to all the yachties out there who posted videos relating to their boating experiences, especially Jennifer and James Hamilton for YouTube videos and blog posts about their adventures on the *Dirona*, their Nordhavn 52.

Team Dusty. I couldn't do without their practical assistance, travelling companionship and moral support.

I am deeply grateful to my beta readers (Anita Marshall, Gael Cresp, Judi Hillyear and Sheila O'Shea) whose feedback gave the manuscript its final polish.

Friends and family members as well as the Friday Writers and the Writers' Lunch Group continue to provide much appreciated feedback and support.

My heartfelt appreciation to all those who have read my other books and posted wonderful comments on Amazon, Goodreads and other sites that have validated and encouraged me as a writer.

Made in the USA
Monee, IL
04 November 2020